CATHAYS CEMETERY CARDIFF

on its 150th Anniversary

Friends of Cathays Cemetery

Published by the Friends of Cathays Cemetery

Designed by Tony Price Associates

Printed by AST Print Group, Cardiff

Acknowledgements

The Friends of Cathays Cemetery are grateful to the following, without whom the production of this book would not have been possible:

The Awards for All Fund for the grant, which has underwritten the cost of publication, and Ageing Well, Age Concern, for their financial assistance.

The National Library of Wales, Glamorgan Archives, Cardiff Library, Landmark Information Group and the Western Mail for permission to reproduce material from their archives. Appropriate accreditations are given against individual items as they appear in the book.

The late Dr Langmead, for his excellent work on Robert G Thomas, and Newport Library, Dr Robin Hawkins and Newport Art Gallery, for granting access to their collections on Robert G Thomas.
Brian Lee for the Preface.
Dr Madeleine Gray, University of Wales, Newport, for the Foreword.
Dr Julian Litten for "The Victorian Funeral" (Chapter 5).
Laura Palmer, Cardiff Council, for "Bats" (part of Chapter 6).
Stephen Howe, National Museum Wales, for "Geology" (part of Chapter 6).

Bereavement Services Division, Cardiff Council, for their unstinting support for this enterprise and for permission to borrow freely from their Trail Guides and other documents.

Members of the Friends who have undertaken the majority of the research and writing and provided many of the illustrations. Individual accreditations are given within the body of the book. Special thanks however go to the members of the Book Committee, Eric R Fletcher, Gordon Hindess and Bill Mosley, for bringing it all together.

Thanks to Tony Price for images used for main cover, inside covers and pages III, iv, x, 81. 82 and 90.

ISBN: 978 0 9562786 09
Title: Cathays Cemetery Cardiff

About this Book

The incentive to produce this book was provided by the approach of the 150th anniversary of the opening of Cathays Cemetery in July 1859. With the Friends of Cathays Cemetery only in the second year of their existence and membership quite small, this was perhaps an ambitious task. It would be fair to say that the enterprise has been a rapid learning process. For example, it was only within about six months of publication that it was determined that this would indeed be a book, as opposed to a booklet.

The objective of the book has been to record the history of this Cadw Grade II listed cemetery, outline its changing role within the community and provide an insight into the contribution to Cardiff's development of people buried in it. Deliberately, no attempt has been made to impose a single style on the writing and presentation. So, with a range of authors, from different backgrounds and with different specialisms, the writing ranges from a factual presentation of the results of archive research to fictionalised tales based on real people and events, related to the Cemetery.

Producing this book has shown that what has been recorded now is only brushing the surface of the stories which need to be told about people who have contributed to Cardiff's history.

Foreword

Cathays Cemetery has always been something of a market leader. When it was established in 1859, London had its 'Magnificent Seven' cemeteries on the edge of the built-up area and Glasgow had its Necropolis, but many urban burials were still taking place in graveyards like the 'tiny churchyard, pestiferous and obscene' in which Lady Dedlock's late lover was buried in Dickens's Bleak House. Nor was Cathays Cemetery only for the dead. Laid out as an arboretum with a wide range of trees and shrubs, the graves deliberately adorned with examples of sculpture and religious symbolism, it was a place for working-class self-education as well as fresh air and exercise, part of Cardiff's network of 'green lungs'.

Cathays Cemetery has also been in the vanguard of the movement to develop cemeteries as heritage sites and educational resources. Genealogists have used tombs and memorials for centuries, and as family history has become more popular so have graveyards and cemeteries. Both historical and wildlife organisations are becoming increasingly aware of the potential of churchyards as repositories of community history and biodiversity. The 'Caring for God's Acre' project in Herefordshire and the Gwent Wildlife Trust's Living Churchyards Project both reflect this – but Cathays was there first!

As an academic historian and a Fellow of the National Museum, I value Cathays Cemetery as a resource. Graveyards have always told the stories of their communities, and much of the history of modern Cardiff can be taught through its memorials. As well as those commemorating famous individuals, there are memorials to social groups which reflect Cardiff's industrial past, memorials to coal magnates and businessmen. Even the divisions in the cemetery are important. The wealthy have crypts and memorials near the main avenues, the paupers have unmarked graves; Anglicans, Catholics and Nonconformists have separate areas – but they are all within its walls. There are monuments erected by public subscription or grateful third parties: for example, one to Louisa Maud Evans, the young girl who died in a freak ballooning accident during the Cardiff Exhibition of 1896 and one to the boxer Jim Driscoll, paid for by the grateful sisters of Nazareth House. Even the actual stones of the memorials are important. Some families brought stone for their monuments from their home areas, and there were different stones which were viewed as appropriate for different social groups. The range of stone types can tell us about the scope of Cardiff's trade and the changing world economic conditions which now make it cheaper to ship (for example) black granite from India rather than Cornwall.

But I also value Cathays Cemetery as a Cardiff resident. It still sits at the heart of the community, its appearance enhanced by the restoration of its railings (which has, ironically, reduced vandalism). It is managed by our Bereavement Services, and the range of skills and qualifications of the staff who work there testifies to its importance. To celebrate Cathays Cemetery is to celebrate not death but life – the life of the community of Cardiff and an oasis of wild life in the city.

Dr Madeleine Gray
Reader in History, University of Wales, Newport

An authority on Welsh religious history, Dr Gray's works include *Images of Piety: the iconography of traditional religion in late medieval Wales* and *The medieval bishop's effigies at Llandaff Cathedral.*

Rhagair

Bu Mynwent Cathays yn fynych iawn yn un arloesol. Pan sefydlwyd hi yn 1859, roedd Llundain eisoes yn meddu ar ei 'Saith Mynwent Ddisglair' ar gyrion yr ardaloedd datblygedig ac roedd gan Glasgow ei Necropolis, ond cynhelid llawer o'r angladdau trefol mewn mynwentydd tebyg i'r "tiny churchyard, pestiferous and obscure" lle y claddwyd cyn-gariad y Fonesig Dedlock yn Bleak House (Charles Dickens). Ni'd bod yn orffwysfa i'r meirw oedd unig swyddogaeth Mynwent Cathays. Roedd yn cynnig cyfle i'r dosbarth gweithiol addysgu eu hunain ac i gerdded a chrwydro wrth fwynhau'r awyr iach oherwydd ei chynllunio'n goedardd gydag ystod eang o goed a llwyni ac enghreifftiau o gerfluniau a symbolaeth grefyddol. Ysgyfaint werdd yng nghanol tref a dinas.

Bu Mynwent Cathays yn arwain y symudiad i ddatblygu mynwentydd fel safleoedd treftadaeth ac adnoddau addysgol. Gwerthfawrogwyd beddau a chofebau gan olrheinwyr achau dros y canrifoedd, a chynyddodd poblogrwydd mynwentydd law yn law â'r diddordeb cynyddol mewn hanes teuluol. Mae sefydliadau hanesyddol a bywyd gwyllt fel ei gilydd yn dod yn fwy a mwy ymwybodol o bosibiliadau claddfeydd fel ffynonellau hanes cymunedol a bio-amrywiaeth. Mae'r cynllun 'Gofal am Erw Duw' yn Swydd Henffordd a'r Prosiect Mynwentydd Byw gan Ymddiriedolaeth Bywyd Gwyllt Gwent yn brawf pellach o hyn – ond achubodd Cathays y blaen arnynt oll!

Fel hanesydd academaidd a Chymrawd yr Amgueddfa Genedlaethol rwy'n ystyried Mynwent Cathays yn adnodd hynod o bwysig. Mae'r mynwentydd bob amser wedi darlunio bywyd eu cymunedau, a gellir dysgu cryn dipyn o hanes Caerdydd trwy gerrig coffa'r fangre hon. Yn ychwanegol at y rhai sy'n coffau unigolion adnabyddus, mae yno gofebau i grwpiau cymdeithasol sy'n adlewyrchu gorffennol diwydiannol Caerdydd, cofebau i wyr busnes a mawrion y diwydiant glo. Mae'r rhaniadau yn y fynwent yn ddiddorol ynddynt eu hunain. Mae claddgelloedd a chofebau'r cyfoethogion ger y prif rodfeydd, beddau di-enw sydd i'r tlodion; hawlia'r Anglicaniaid, Catholigion a'r Anghydffurfiwyr eu hardaloedd eu hunain –ond mae pawb o fewn y muriau. Mae yno gofgolofnau a godwyd gan gyfraniadau'r cyhoedd neu gyfeillion gwerthfawrogol un, er enghraifft i Louisa Maud Evans, y ferch ifanc a laddwyd mewn damwain balwn yn ystod Arddangosfa Caerdydd yn 1896 ac un i'r paffiwr Jim Driscoll, rhodd gan Chwiorydd diolchgar Nazareth House. Mae hyd yn oed gerrig y cofebau yn ddiddorol a dadlennol. Cludodd rhai teuluoedd gerrig o'u cynefin hwy ac mae yno amrywiol gerrig a ystyrid yn briodol i'r gwahanol grwpiau cymdeithasol. Mae'r amrediad o feini yn ddrych o amrywiaeth masnach Caerdydd a'r newidiadau yn yr amodau economaidd byd-eang sy'n ei gwneud yn rhatach (er enghraifft) i fewnforio gwenithfaen du o India yn hytrach nag o Gernyw.

Ond mi rydw i hefyd, fel un o drigolion Caerdydd, yn gwerthfawrogi Mynwent Cathays. Mae'n parhau'n ganolog i'r gymuned, ei golwg wedi gwella o ganlyniad i adnewyddu'r rheiliau o'i chwmpas (sydd, yn eironig ddigon, wedi lleihau fandaliaeth). Fe'i rheolir gan ein Gwasanaeth Galar, ac mae'r cyfoeth o sgiliau a chymwysterau'r gweithlu yno yn tystio i'w phwysigrwydd. Dathlu bywyd yn hytrach na marwolaeth yw dathlu Mynwent Cathays – bywyd cymuned Caerdydd a gwerddon o fywyd gwyllt yn y ddinas.

Dr Madeleine Gray
Prifysgol Cymru, Casnewydd

A hithau'n awdurdod ar hanes crefyddol Cymru mae gweithiau Dr. Gray yn cynnwys *Images of Piety: the iconography of traditional religion in late medieval Wales* a *The medieval bishop's effigies at Llandaff Cathedral.*

Contents

Preface

The contributors to this excellent book are to be congratulated on giving us a fascinating insight into one of Cardiff's most important and largest landmarks.

Being brought up in the Cathays area, the cemetery was a regular haunt of mine and I often visited the grave of Peerless Jim Driscoll to see his boxing gloves that were incased in a glass bowl on his grave – that was until some despicable person stole them in the 1950s. Another grave I used to visit – still do from time to time – is that of little Louisa Maud Evans who at the great Cardiff Fine Art, Industrial and Maritime Exhibition of 1896 tragically died in a controversial ballooning accident.

The one hundred or so acres covering Cathays Cemetery contain thousands of memorials of long gone Cardiffians some more famous than others. People who helped to make our beloved Cardiff what it is today. John Cory, for instance, the famed ship-owner originally from Padstow in Cornwall whose rapidly expanding company, in the days when Coal was King, provided hundreds of jobs for Cardiffians and whose offices were on the corner of Mount Stuart Square and James Street in Cardiff's Docklands. Another memorial is to Charles Vachell who built the first house in Queen Street, then known as Crockherbtown, and who was elected Mayor on two occasions (1849 and 1855). And who, because of his concern over the poor living conditions of some of the people in the town, played a big part in the implementation of the Public Health Act (1848).

A not so well known memorial is that of gentleman rider Joseph Butler Jones who held up the sporting tradition of Cardiff and who was known on the racecourse as 'Joe the Crwys.' He had many notable successes at the old Heath Racecourse and later at Cardiff's Ely Racecourse. It was at Ely Racecourse on his grey Cabin Boy that he won the Cardiff Open Steeplechase a race from which the Welsh Grand National now run at Chepstow is derived. There is also a memorial to William James Tatem, better known as Lord Glanely, who was one of the most famous racehorse owners in the history of the Turf. This forceful character, known as 'Old Guts and Gaiters', won all of racing's classics. Not bad going for someone who started off as clerk in Cardiff Docks before going on to form his own shipping company in 1909.

As you are about to find out this unique book covers many other aspects of Cathays Cemetery from Victorian Funerals to Nature and Biodiversity. It will be of great interest to Cardiffians young and old alike and should be made available to all Cardiff Schools so that pupils can learn something about an area of an ever changing Cardiff that is rarely written about.

Brian Lee

As Cardiffians well know, Brian is the author of many best-selling local history books and his weekly *Cardiff Remembered* column in the *Cardiff Post* is very popular.

Cyflwyniad

Rhaid llongyfarch y cyfranwyr i'r llyfr hwn am roi i ni olwg gyfareddol ar un o gyrchfannau pwysicaf a mwyaf helaeth Caerdydd. Oherwydd mai yn ardal Cathays y magwyd fi, roedd y fynwent yn atyniad cyson ac ymwelais lawer tro â bedd yr Anghymarol Jim Driscoll i weld ei fenyg paffio mewn cawg gwydr ar ei fedd – hynny yw, nes i ryw berson gwrth-gymdeithasol eu dwyn yn ystod y pumdegau. Bedd arall yr ymwelais ag ef – ac sy'n fy nenu o dro i dro o hyd – yw un Louisa Maud Evans a fu farw mor drychinebus mewn damwain balwn ddadleuol yn ystod Arddangosfa Celfyddyd Gain, Diwydiant a Morwrol Caerdydd yn 1896.

Mae'r can cyfer mwy neu lai o dir Mynwent Cathays yn leoliad i filoedd o gofebau i drigolion Caerdydd y gorffennol, rhai ohonynt yn enwocach na'i gilydd. Pobl a wnaeth ein hannwyl Gaerdydd yr hyn ydyw heddiw. Dyna i chi John Cory, y perchennog llongau adnabyddus o Padstow yng Nghernyw, a greodd gannoedd lawer o swyddi i weithwyr Caerdydd yn y cyfnod pan oedd Glo yn Frenin. Roedd gan ei gwmni llewyrchus swyddfeydd ar gornel Sgwâr Mount Stuart a James Street yn ardal y dociau. Ceir cofeb arall i Charles Vachell a adeiladodd y tŷ cyntaf yn Heol y Frenhines, a elwid bryd hynny yn Crockherbtown, ac a etholwyd yn Faer ar ddau achlysur (1849 a 1855). Ef hefyd, oherwydd ei gonsyrn am amodau byw rhai o dlodion y dref, a chwaraeodd ran amlwg mewn gweithredu Deddf Iechyd Cyhoeddus, 1848.

Cofeb llai adnabyddus yw'r un i'r boneddwr o joci Joseph Butler Jones a adnabyddid ar y maes rasio ceffylau fel 'Joe the Crwys'. Bu'n aml ei lwyddiannau ar hen faes rasio'r Heath ac yn ddiweddarach ar faes Trelai. Yn Nhrelai, ar ei geffyl Cabin Boy yr enillodd ras agored Ffos a Pherth Caerdydd-rhagflaenydd Grand National Cymru a gynhelir yng Nghasgwent yn flynyddol bellach. Yno hefyd fe welir cofeb i William James Tatem sy'n fwy adnabyddus fel yr Arglwydd Glanely, un o'r perchenogion ceffylau rasus enwocaf yn hanes y diwydiant. Enillodd y cymeriad egniol hwn, 'Old Guts and Gaiters' ar dafod leferydd bob un o glasuron y byd rasio. Tipyn o gamp i fachgen a ddringodd o fod yn glerc yn Nociau Caerdydd i sefydlu ei gwmni llongau ei hun yn 1909.

Mae'r llyfr unigryw hwn, fel gwelwch, yn cofnodi agweddau eraill o hanes Mynwent Cathays o Angladdau Fictorianaidd i Natur a Bioamrywiaeth. Bydd o ddiddordeb i bobl Caerdydd yn hen ac ifanc fel ei gilydd a dylai fod ar gael i holl ysgolion y Brifddinas er mwyn galluogi'r disgyblion i ddysgu am ardal o'r Gaerdydd gyfnewidiol gyfredol nas ysgrifennir amdani yn aml.

Brian Lee

Fel y gŵyr trigolion Caerdydd, mae Brian yn awdur llu o lyfrau hanes lleol poblogaidd ac mae ei golofn wythnosol *Cardiff Remembered* yn y *Cardiff Post* un boblogaidd iawn.

CHAPTER ONE

History of the Cemetery – The Land

Why the need for a new Cemetery?

Cardiff was a town with two parishes, St John the Baptist and St Mary the Virgin, [St John's Church being the Chapel of Ease for the parish of St Mary and serving the combined inhabitants of both parishes for Baptisms and Marriages]. But since the great flood of 1607, when the ruins and burial ground of old St Mary's were flooded, the churchyard of St John's Church was the place of burial for the majority of the inhabitants who were not of the nonconformist persuasion. The churchyard, which extended for a distance of 116ft from the south porch and was approximately 90ft wide, had been sufficient for the joint parishes.

According to the printed notes in the census summaries the population of Cardiff multiplied between 1801 and 1831 as a direct result of the increase in trade, as tonnage on the Glamorganshire Canal increased due to the rise in the industrial output in Merthyr Tydfil. The increase in the next 10 years to 1841 was due to an agricultural depression in the neighbouring villages.

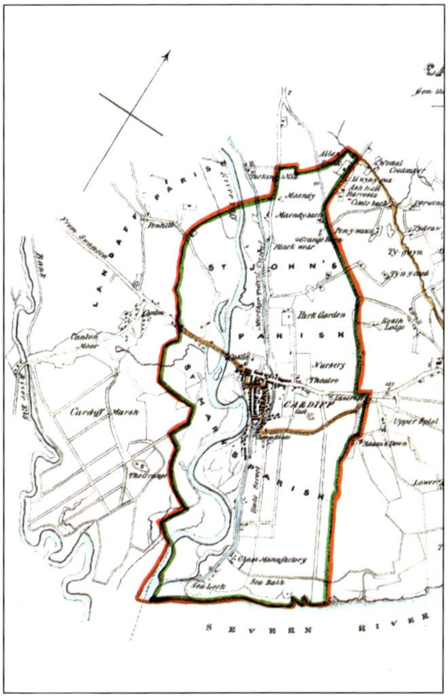

Map of the Borough of Cardiff in 1832
HM Government copyright waived'

Census Years	1801	1811	1821	1831	1841	1851	1861	1871
Population	1870	2457	3521	6187	10077	18351	32951	39536
Acreage	2321	2321	2321	2321	2321	2321	3159	3159
Acreage under Water	562	562	562	562	562	562	562	562
Adjusted Acreage	1759	1759	1759	1759	1759	1759	2597	2597
% Pop to Acreage	1	1.5	2	3.5	5.75	10.5	12.6	15

Population for St John's Parish from 1801 to 1871 [after 1851 it includes the parish of St Mary]

Because of the growth of the population as outlined above the burial ground was inadequate for the burial needs of the borough and town of Cardiff. Therefore in 1809 the Vicar, churchwardens and the inhabitants (town population) petitioned the bishop to extend the churchyard, the borough having freely given an area of 193 sq yards.

Further Expansion of Old Churchyard

As the population of the joint parishes grew by 50% in the period 1811 to 1821 the Churchwardens [William Vachell and William Bird], looking to the future, purchased the garden that was owned by John Richards which bordered the existing church yard. Having petitioned the bishop for this area to be enclosed and added to the Burial Ground for the joint parishes it was duly consecrated in 1822.

Detail of the map by John Wood circa late 1830s
Courtesy of the Archivist of Glamorgan Archives

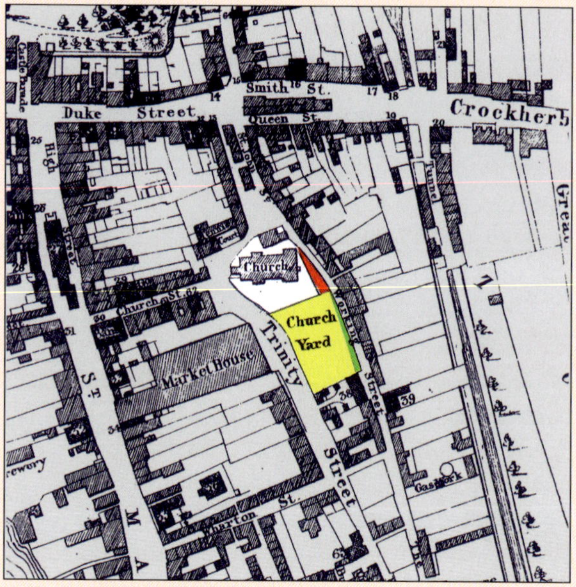

KEY

The white area is the extent of the medieval church yard to 1809; the triangle in Red denotes the 1809 extension; the 1822 extension is coloured in Yellow; the additional triangular area in 1830 is in Green.

This extended the area for burial south of the old boundary wall by 148 ft and by 96 feet wide from Trinity Street to an area called "Old Troy". Even this would be insufficient for the rapidly increasing population of Cardiff which grew by 75% between 1821 and 1831, so the burial ground was extended by the purchase of a triangular plot that took in an area called "Little Troy". This extension was consecrated on 30th October 1830 and became the final extent of the united Burial Ground for the parishes of St John and St Mary the Virgin [then newly re-established].

As the development of the port of Cardiff, the ship canal and the railway was undertaken by Lord Bute the population steadily grew to the levels recorded in 1841. The collieries in Aberdare opened by 1851 and produced excellent steam coal which was shipped from Cardiff all over the world. These exports from the Aberdare and Rhondda valleys, along with the increase in the iron and steel from Merthyr Tydfil and the Taff Vale would be the cause of the continuing increase in the population of Cardiff.

With the growing population as a direct result of the growing economic success of Cardiff the town council along with the parish vestry looked to the future and obtained a grant of land on 9th November 1836 from Lord Bute that adjoined Whitmore Lane to the east of the town. It was one acre in size and consecrated in 1848. The civil and parish authorities may have felt that this was sufficient for the burial requirements of the borough, along with those Chapels that had their own burial grounds, but in 1849 the town succumbed to an outbreak of Cholera and as a result 360 people died, so this new burial ground was soon deemed to be filled and the town council would be looking for more ground.

The cholera outbreak was part of an epidemic that affected the major cities in England

and Wales and Parliament in 1852 had passed the first Burial Act under which church and chapel burial grounds could be closed to new burials and the local authorities could be constituted a Burial Board. Cardiff Town Council was constituted a Burial Board under the 1855 Act on 30th Jan 1856 with the purpose of providing for requisite places of burial for the inhabitants of the parishes of St John and St Mary in the Borough of Cardiff.

On 26th June 1854 the Town Council made an order that the Burial Grounds were to be closed as follows:

> *Forthwith*
> *St John and St Mary; in Ebenezer Chapel; in Zion Chapel; in the Bethany Baptist Chapel and in the Tabernacle.*

A later order in 1856 extended the prohibition to include:

> *St John's Churchyard and St Mary's additional churchyard; the cemetery in Ebenezer Chapel, Zion Burial grounds and in the Tabernacle and Bethany Baptist Burial grounds' (except in graves that can be opened to the depth of 5 feet or in vaults or brick graves, except for the burial of husbands, wives, parents or unmarried children of those previously buried).*

The prohibition was further extended to include the Cemetery at Whitmore Lane (Adamsdown). Although the order to close the existing burial grounds was for immediate execution, it was to be delayed until any new provision for burials was available.

Even with the delay in imposing the order there was still a need for new burials:

> *"for the inhabitants of the several parishes of St John the Baptist and St Mary comprising the borough, the council ordered the Mayor or the ex Mayor Alderman CC Williams and Messrs Lewis Reece and Griffiths Phillips to undertake to look out for a new burial ground and that it was to be no less than 20 acres and not exceeding 40 acres ... and to be within 4 miles of the town of Cardiff".*

Advertisements were published in the three Cardiff newspapers.

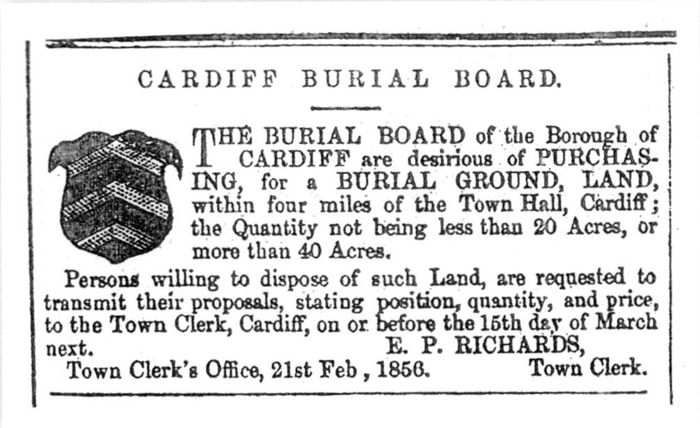

CARDIFF BURIAL BOARD.

THE BURIAL BOARD of the Borough of CARDIFF are desirious of PURCHASING, for a BURIAL GROUND, LAND, within four miles of the Town Hall, Cardiff; the Quantity not being less than 20 Acres, or more than 40 Acres.

Persons willing to dispose of such Land, are requested to transmit their proposals, stating position, quantity, and price, to the Town Clerk, Cardiff, on or before the 15th day of March next.

E. P. RICHARDS,
Town Clerk's Office, 21st Feb , 1856. Town Clerk.

Cardiff and Merthyr Times, 1856
Courtesy of the Cardiff Capital Collection

Purchase of New Cemetery

The endeavours of the Burial Board resulted on 7th March 1859 in the purchase of 30 acres from Wyndham William Lewis of the Heath, Cardiff for £4,500. They consisted of arable farm-land situated just beyond the Borough marker, about 1½ miles to the north east of the town and within the parish of St John the Baptist.

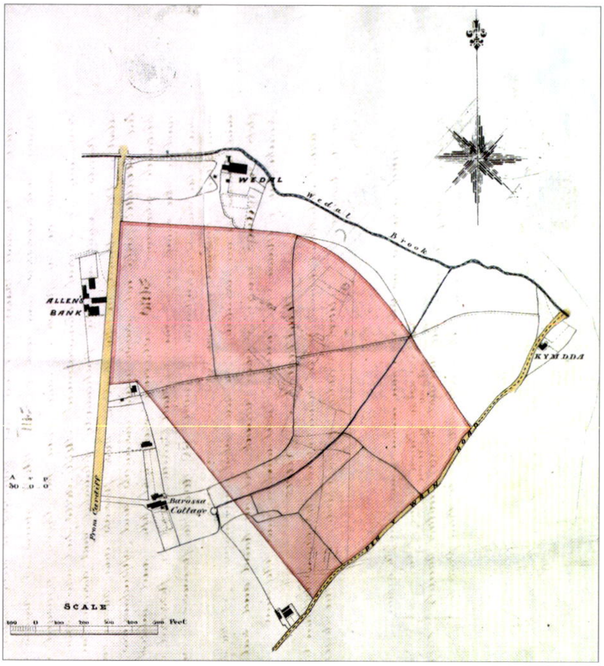

Plan of the area purchased in 1859

By permission of Llyfrgell Genedlaethol Cymru / The National Library of Wales

The cemetery was consecrated on Friday 28th October 1859 by the Bishop of Llandaff, and, although the weather was unpleasant the Chapel was full. Among the guests [apart from the church and borough officials] were Mr R G Thomas of Newport, the architect who had designed the three chapels and the buildings, Mr Thomas Waring who had superintended the building of the chapels and Mr John Palmer, the resident Clerk of Works, who had superintended the roads and approaches.

The following is the description of the new cemetery from the article in *The Cardiff Times* on Saturday 5th November 1859:

> *"...Having walked as far as Crwys Farm, you turn to the right, and a short walk along Pen-y-wain (now Fairoak) Road' brings you to the cemetery, ... The approach is by a large archway with carriage entrance and gate and it has also gates at each side for foot passengers. The archway is ornamented with the arms of the Corporation of Cardiff, the Diocese of Llandaff and C.C. Williams Esq., the Mayor of Cardiff under whose auspices the buildings have been erected. Immediately opposite this entrance and on the south portion of the ground are situated the two chapels for the Church of England and for Nonconformist Protestants. The chapels form the wings of an extensive group of buildings of which the porches and vestries form a connection, and the central part of which is formed by a tower and spire. The chapels are entered by the porches and carriage porches are also provided under which hearses will draw up. The chapels are handsome buildings, in the Gothic style of Architecture. Each is calculated to accommodate for 150 persons. They are fitted up with pews and reading desks of stained deal and varnished. The roofs are open to the rafters which are stained similarly to the seats and the supports ribs, which are moulded, terminate on handsomely carved corbels of freestone. The windows are all traceried, those at each end being very large and handsome, and we hope that stained glass will eventually be substituted for the plain glass now fixed.*

With this addition the interior will have nothing to be desired. The central portion of the group is formed by a tower and spire as already stated. The spire when completed will rise above 100 feet in height and will be a conspicuous feature in the landscape. The whole of grounds are laid out with carriage drives and footpaths of various widths. The central drive has an avenue of horse-chestnut trees, and forms the boundary between the consecrated and unconsecrated portions of the ground; after dividing the ground it terminates in a separate entrance from Plucca Lane. Near this path the Roman Catholic chapel is situated. It is smaller than the others but similar in character and the portion of the ground allotted to the Roman Catholics is provided with a gate for their especial use. The whole of the grounds have been well stocked with trees and shrubs, and flower beds have been formed opposite the chapels, and around the keeper's lodge. This part of the contract was performed by Mr Matthews of the Cardiff nursery, and we have no doubt that in a short time, not only will the cemetery have a pretty appearance but that it will form the principal walk of the inhabitants of the town of Cardiff..."

On 19th November 1859, *The Cardiff Times* also reported that the Roman Catholic Chapel was blessed on Sunday 2nd November by Rev Laurence Gastaldi DD, Rector of St David's Cardiff, with the Rev Fathers Lewis Costa and Michael Garrelli assisting.

The article goes on to state that Mr Roberts, a printer in Cardiff, who entered the chapel either before or after the ceremony against a prohibition that the officiating priest had made before the Blessing (due to the size of the crowd, which was estimated at 1200). This annoyed a part of the crowd, who reacted with violence towards Mr Roberts and were restrained by the Christian conduct of the priest.

"On the following Friday Father Costa had to go to the Town Hall to state the case against Mr Roberts before the Mayor; the case however, was dismissed but Mr Roberts was reprimanded by the magistrate" [*St Peter's Parish Magazine*, 1923, page 322].

Expansion of New Cemetery

The cemetery although of 30 acres was sufficient for the Borough of Cardiff east of the River Taff because the area to the west of the river was in the Parish of Llandaff and their burial ground was around the Cathedral. However in 1876 the committee recommended that it was desirable to acquire more land that adjoined the west side of the cemetery from the trustees of the late Wyndham W Lewis and lying between the present grounds and that recently purchased from Miss Mary Wood. Additional land of about 4 acres was also bought from the Wyndham Lewis Estate adjoining the present consecrated portion of the cemetery, bounded by the Rhymney Railway on the east and a brook on the north. This was purchased on 3rd July 1878 but only 3 acres were consecrated on 9th March 1903, the remainder being used for nonconformist burials.

In 1879 the area used for Roman Catholic burials had been exhausted so the Borough Surveyor was directed to prepare a plan showing the proposed way of laying out the adjacent land recently purchased in order that a portion be set apart for Roman Catholic burials.

Later that year due to the many burials the Committee recommended that Advertisements be placed in the Cardiff Papers, that all graves not purchased within the time specified by the Burial Board Act, viz 14 years for adults and 8 years for children, would again be used for the burial of other parties.

The Borough Authorities having experienced the problems of providing sufficient burial grounds during the early growth of the Town and Borough of Cardiff, looked ahead as the population was still growing at a tremendous rate. In the 20 years from 1851 to 1871 the population had grown from 18,351 to 39,356. So on 15th May 1879 the Town Clerk was instructed to write to Mr Corbett, Agent to the Bute Estate, that the additional land of 11 acres, which was the remaining land of Crwys Brychan Farm, was to be purchased from Lord Bute.

Temporary Recreation Ground

The area acquired was not immediately used for burial purposes, and the following are extracts dealing with this section of the cemetery purchased from the Bute Estate in 1879, from an unpublished book, compiled in 1926, on the Parks and Gardens of Cardiff by the then Superintendent of Gardens, Andrew A Pettigrew.

> *'Alderman Jones, replying to the debate, said, … "referring to the stress which had been laid upon the necessity of first providing recreation grounds for Roath, that the 11½ acres of land which had been acquired for the Cemetery enlargement (at Cathays) might be used as a park for Roath until it was required for the Cemetery, which should not be for some year." '*

The above suggestion that a part of the land acquired for the extension of the new Cemetery at Cathays, and not immediately wanted for burial purposes, might be used for recreation until so required, had been made by Alderman Jones at the Council of 8th July 1878 when the question of proceeding with the acquisition of the commons was under consideration. The question cropped up again at a meeting of the council held on 10th March 1879, when Cllr R Davies made the same suggestion:

> *"Taking into consideration the increase in the population, he thought that if they went into the matter they would find that, after allotting space for burial purposes sufficient to meet the requirements of the next twenty years, they would have 8 to 10 acres available for some other purpose, and the purpose he proposed was recreation. This could be done at little cost, as the drainage could be made suitable for burial purposes, and when the land was required, but few alterations would be necessary."*

Other members were in agreement with him, though Alderman Bowen, the Chairman of the Burial Board, "did object to a recreation ground next to a cemetery." The matter was eventually referred to the Burial Board Committee. Nothing, however could be done until the ground plans had been prepared and considered, and then, at a meeting of that committee held on the ground on 22nd April 1881, it was decided to recommend to the Council:

> *"That the remainder of the land between Pen-y-wain (now Fairoak) and Whitchurch Roads … be retained in hand, and be devoted to recreation purposes until required for interments."*

The paragraph was challenged when the transactions of the Committee were submitted to the Council on 13th June 1881 and the opposition almost proved too strong. However in the end the opposition's amendment was defeated by 16 votes to 12. The original motion was thereupon carried.

Following this decision, an announcement appeared in the advertisement columns of the local Press on 18th July 1881, as below:

Borough of Cardiff

Notice

The ground adjoining the Cemetery will be opened to the public for recreation purposes on and after Monday next, the 18th inst., between the hours of 8 a.m. and 9.30 p.m., daily. Free. By order, F.R. Greenhill, Clerk Town Hall Cardiff, 15th July 1881.

So Cardiff had its very own recreation ground at last – if only of a temporary character. Its area was approximately 10 acres, at that end of the Cemetery, part of which is now occupied by the Cathays Library.

Says the *Illustrated Guide to Cardiff* (1882):

"The Cathays population are indebted to the Cardiff Corporation for a recreation ground in which seats have been placed for the convenience for visitors. Visitors, however, are not numerous, and the benevolent intentions of the Corporate body have met with anything but a flattering reception from that portion of their constituents."

Which may be very true of the ground as a "walk," but as a playing field it was certainly much appreciated by the youth of those days.

As I do not intend to refer further to this recreation ground, I may here state shortly its subsequent history. In 1887 its size was considerably reduced for the purpose of extending the burial ground; the Burial Board Committee had in fact asked Council for the whole to be closed but this was refused. In 1888 the same Committee proposed that the Parks Committee should undertake responsibility for its care, but that Committee objected on the score of unnecessary expense. Finally, the following resolution of the Burial Board Committee of 5th February 1895 [confirmed later by Council] marks the end of the New Cemetery Recreation Ground:

"That in the opinion of this Board the time has arrived for utilizing the Recreation Ground for Burial Board purposes, and the same shall therefore be forthwith laid out, formed and planted accordingly."

At a committee meeting on 19th May 1881 school children were allowed to use the land at Pen-y-wain and Whitchurch Roads and adjoining the Rhymney Railway for Whitsun Treats. Such was the expanse of grass that Mr Thomas Morgan paid £15 for the year of 1882 to graze his sheep. This of course saved money as it meant that it would not need cutting manually. This arrangement was not for more than a year as the manager was soon selling the grass and having to employ men to cut it. When in 1883 the army requested the use of the recreation field for an encampment from 26th May to 21st June the request was declined. On 5th February 1895 it was decided that this area should be used for nonconformist burials. So the area of the Cemetery that is shown on the all the maps from 1887 onwards was complete and survives today and it was hoped to be sufficient for the needs of the Borough well into the 20th Century.

Jewish Burial Grounds

The Jewish burial grounds were firstly situated at Highfield just outside the borough in 1841 and at the two synagogues in the town, Edwards Place and Cathedral Road. In 1887 a group from the Jewish community applied for a separate burial ground and in April of that year a deputation speaking for the majority of the community met with several members of the council to resolve the problem. They did not require a separate burial ground however as there was still 39 years burial space left at the Synagogue in Edwards Place, while at the Cathedral Road Synagogue there was space for the next 28 years. It was left to the deputation to resolve the problem and the case was subsequently dropped.

Crematorium

The subject of a crematorium as an alternative to burials was first discussed at the committee meeting of 2nd April 1895 where it was resolved that the Architect to the Burial Board be requested to make a report to be presented at a special meeting with a view to expediting the erection of a crematorium. This was to replace the one on Flat Holm, the island in the Bristol Channel some 3 to 4 miles from the Borough of Cardiff. The special meeting was duly held on 17th May 1895 but no decision was reached. However by the meeting on 3rd March 1896 it was resolved that papers for and against the crematorium could be left at the cemetery office, burial board office, town hall and the free libraries.

At a meeting on 13th September 1896 the committee resolved to follow the advice of the Town Clerk regarding the crematorium and accompanying the Borough Engineer they visited the site on the northern boundary midway between the Rhymney Railway and the Allensbank Road which was considered the best location for its erection. It was resolved that a plan be shown at the meeting showing the plot. On 20th October 1896 the committee, having agreed in principle to the building of the crematorium, asked the Borough Surveyor to draw up plans for a full council meeting; this resolution was passed even though many members said that they would vote against the proposal at the full council meeting. The proposal was referred to the Secretary of State whose reply raised many issues so that on 29th June 1897 the proposal was referred to the Town Clerk to reply to the Secretary of State as required by the Cardiff Corporation Act of 1894. The Council did not again consider the matter of a crematorium until the middle of the 20th Century when the present crematorium was built at Thornhill.

Further Cemetery Extension

As a result of the economic boom, in Cardiff, during the last decade of the 19th century, the population was to grow from 128,918 in 1891 to 164,333 by 1901 which was without doubt an amazing growth in ten years. This was to put a strain on the provision of burial grounds and so as early as February 1896 the Burial Board began looking at extending the existing provision by asking the Borough Engineer to prepare a plan and to ascertain the acreage of the land from the present cemetery to the Water Works filter beds and bounded by the

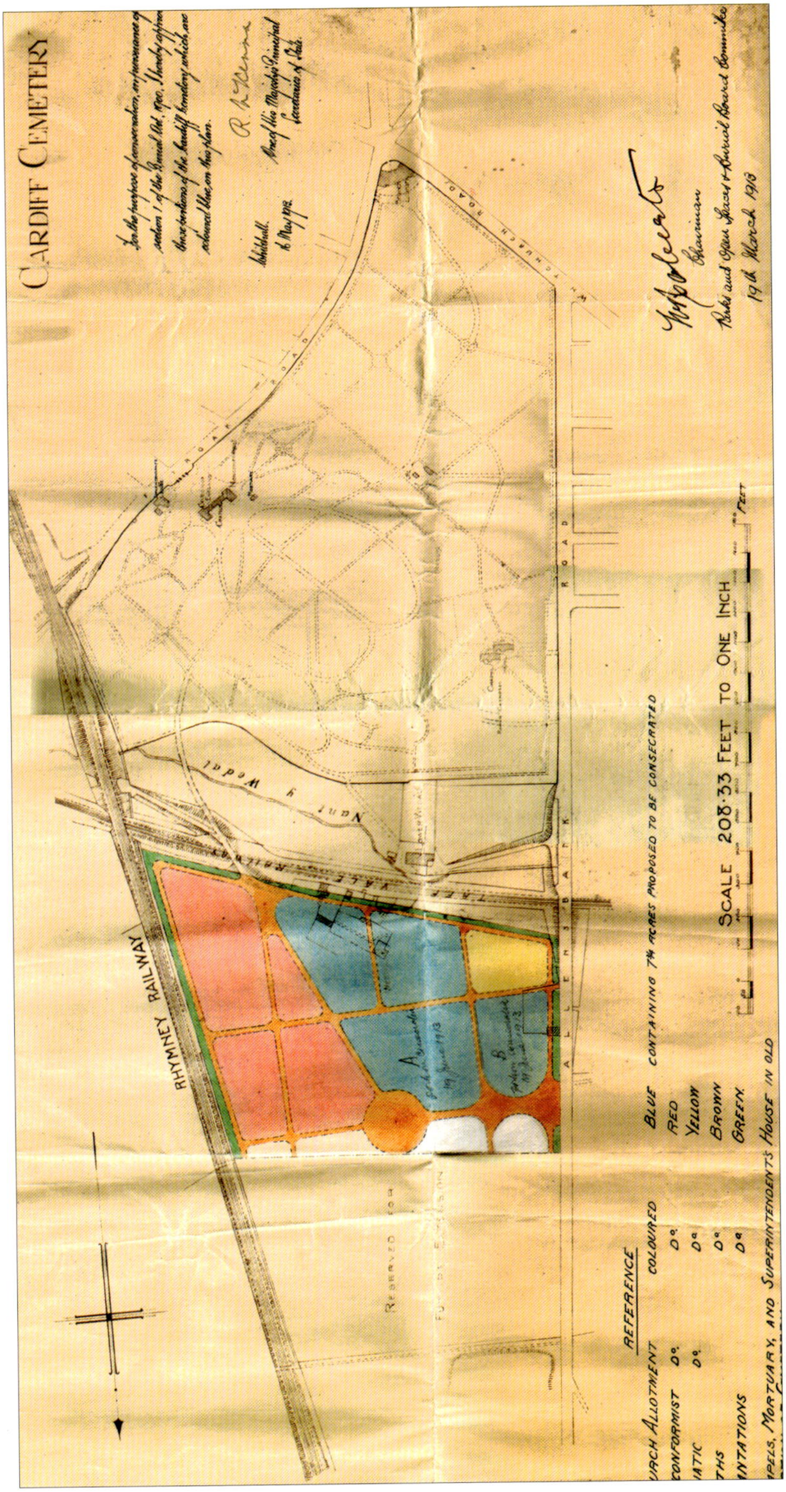

Illustration plan, 1913
Bereavement Services

Rhymney Railway on the East and Llanishen (Allensbank) Road on the West. This land was occupied as Lower Wedal Farm.

The committee also visited other sites around the Borough as follows:

- Northern side of Cowbridge Road opposite the Ely industrial school.
- Land south of Fairwater Road and east of the Fairwater brook and extending to the Great Western Railway.
- The land on the Llantrisant road between Baynton House Llandaff and the Taff Vale Penarth Branch Railway.

The committee recommended buying either the land adjoining the present cemetery or the land at Ely opposite the Ely industrial school.

After the enquires made by the Borough Engineer the committee at the meeting of 9th July1896 resolved to accept Lord Tredegar's offer of about 35 acres of land adjoining the present cemetery at £350 per acre. At the next meeting a further 10 acres, the land occupied by the Wedal farm was offered, and accepted, at £400 per acre from the Misses Lewis. It was also resolved at that meeting to apply to H M Treasury for permission to borrow the amount of £17,800 for the purpose of purchasing 45 acres of land from Lord Tredegar and the Misses Lewis for enlarging the Cardiff Cemetery. Upon adoption of this resolution it was amended so that the land could be used for allotments for the district of Cathays, until such time as it was required for burials.

The Borough of Cardiff owned the Mount on Llanishen Road and it adjoined the land that was being purchased from Lord Tredegar, so the tenant Mr R R Alward was informed that his tenancy would not be renewed after 2nd January 1897. After many meetings and discussion about the compensation due to the tenants, Wedal Farm was finally purchased from Lord Tredegar on 10th May 1898 for £12,143.

This extra area of acres was again for both the Established Church and Nonconformists and the area of Wedal Farm was laid out for burials in January 1901. The Established Church section (in blue on the adjoining plan) was consecrated on 1904. The other sections have been used by the Nonconformists and other faiths.

Nicholas Davey

CHAPTER TWO

History of the Cemetery – The Buildings

The Protestant Chapels

In the description of Cardiff in the 1871 Post Office Directory, the Chapel designs were chosen as the result of a competition and the successful ones were joint designs by Mr R G Thomas, now Architect in Adelaide, and Mr Thomas Waring, Surveyor to the Board of Health of Cardiff at the time.

Having searched the minutes of Cardiff Borough Council, the Burial Board, the Cemetery Committee and *The Cardiff Times* from 1847 to 1859, I can find no reference to a competition but the description in *The Cardiff Times* of the act of consecration does say:

> *"The whole of the chapels and buildings have been erected from the designs of, and superintended by Mr R G Thomas, Architect of Cardiff and Newport, the roads and approaches and engineering works generally have been superintended by Mr Thomas Waring, the surveyor to the Board of Health, at Cardiff. The resident clerk of works is Mr John Palmer."*

Robert George Thomas (RGT)

He was born on the 16th February 1820, in the Parish of St Dunstan's in the West in the city of London, the eldest son of Robert and Mary Thomas. His father had been born in November 1781 at a farm called Rhantregwnwyn in the Parish of Llanymynech, which straddles the counties of Montgomeryshire and Shropshire.

R G Thomas

Courtesy of South Australia Archives

At the age 21 RGT's father moved to London, where he set up a Printing House in Fleet Street, establishing himself as a Law Stationer. He married Mary Harris, the daughter of George and Mary Harris on 8th January 1818 at Holy Rood Church in Southampton, the church in which she had been baptised on 30th August 1787.

As well as RGT, Robert and Mary's other children were Frances (Amelia) baptised on 14th November 1818, William Kyffin baptised on 4th November 1821, Mary born 30th August 1823, Helen

Mantegani born 6th July 1825 and Alfred born on 22nd February 1827 [but died by June 1827].

Influenced by the writings of Edward Gibbon Wakefield, RGT's father bought 134 acres (54 ha) in the proposed province in South Australia and emigrated there in 1836 with his family, 6 months after RGT himself had arrived there with the first surveying team.

RGT had been articled to George Strickland Kingston, the colony's proposed Deputy Surveyor who was employed in surveying, preparing maps, designing prefabricated buildings and planning the principle town, which on 28th December 1836 was named Adelaide. RGT may well have drawn the first map of the City of Adelaide in 1838. He worked on various projects including the Birmingham Waterworks and for various employers including Colonel William Light, the colony's Surveyor General, who employed him after he left the colonial surveying office, in 1838. After Colonel Light's death in 1839 he worked for George Strickland Kingston's firm, where he met William James from Monmouthshire with whom he went into partnership in January 1845.

In December 1845 they were appointed surveyors to the Adelaide Mining Association which was involved in the Burra "Monster" Copper Mine, which was to secure Adelaide's future. It is however surprising that, being involved in this quickly developing industry, RGT and James decided to return to Britain, where due to "Railway Mania" surveyors were in much demand. James had connections with Monmouthshire, his father being County Surveyor there, so they decided to settle in that county where they arrived in 1846 having sailed from Australia on the Cleveland on 5 April 1846.

RGT settled and worked in Newport and in 1851 he was living in 23 Commercial Street as an Engineer and Architect. James worked as a Building Contractor in the company of James and Parry who were based in Romilly Crescent in Cardiff. RGT and James worked together on some projects such as:

Ebenezer Chapel, Charles Street, Cardiff
Gordon Hindess

- Training College for the National Education Society, Carmarthen: July 1847
- Also in 1847 to 1848: Museum at Caerleon; Bank in Usk; Parsonage at Carmarthen

During his time in Wales RGT was designing in a variety of styles, as can be seen in the folio of his works in the Newport Art Gallery, e.g. the design for the Baptist Chapel in Newport [possibly Commercial Street or Charles Street] is in English Perpendicular/Gothic style but attached to it is one in the Romanesque style.

When James and Parry won the contract for the building of the Ebenezer Independent Chapel in Charles Street, RGT's design is in this hybrid style as shown in the Newport Art Gallery folio. This Chapel is well known for the many coloured stones that make up its walls, not requested from the heads of the countries where they come from [as an urban myth suggests] but from the huge mounds of ballast that were deposited alongside the Cardiff docks from the many ships that were using the port at the time.

Thomas Waring [TW]

He was born in Royston and was employed as Surveyor and Engineer to Cardiff, Canton and Roath Local Boards of Health, as well as Cardiff Rural District. He was responsible for large numbers of houses built between 1874 and 1890. In 1861 he is described as the Architect of the Cardiff Baths, Guildford Crescent, in the company papers registered that year. The total cost of the chapels and the manager's house was £5,200 (£240,000 at today's prices).

Episcopalian [left hand] and Nonconformist [right hand] Chapels, 1905

Front of Chapels from the South-west, circa 1905

Front of Chapels, 1905

Cemetery Gates, Fairoak Road, circa 1905

Cemetery Lodge, 1905

All images Courtesy of Cardiff Capital Collection

RGT left Britain in 1861 and was in Adelaide at the time of his last payment of £35 for his work in connection with the chapels. From then on TW continued in the employ of the cemetery authorities being variously described as Surveyor or Architect, depending on what was required of him.

The Need for Repairs

It was not long after the buildings were opened that the problems of the site of the chapels being North-facing on an East-West alignment [and on the top of a ridge of land exposed to the extremes of the gales that swept over it] became apparent.

At the committee meeting of 7th November 1861 the Lodge Keeper, William Timms, reported that due to the recent weather the chuting (guttering) and slating of the Episcopal Chapel needed to be repaired which TW was instructed to do. However the same work was required in September 1868 when several slates had been blown off and damaged the chuting sufficiently for a new piece to be required.

When in August 1862 Mr Timms reported that the outer doors of the Chapels and the Cemetery Gates should be painted and The Lodge papered it was TW who was asked to prepare the specification; when Mr James Prosser won the tender it was TW who was asked to ensure that it was carried out in the spring of 1863. This work was repeated in 1869, but TW also inspected the gates with a view to making them more effective against trespassers – who were increasing to such a extent that the cemetery manager was instructed to summon them before the town magistrates.

The Lodge Keeper and TW worked together on a lot of suggestions for improving the chapels and in December 1864 it was Mr Timms who reported that the chapel roofs had been damaged in the gales that had battered Cardiff; TW was directed to repair them immediately as Architect.

The Cemetery Manager also made several suggestions regarding drainage and the building of toilets behind the Protestant chapels both of which TW reported on and in due course they were adopted. The toilets where later replaced in 1893 following a resolution to that effect at a committee meeting on 9th December 1892.

The Roman Catholic Chapel

This chapel, also designed by Robert G Thomas and Thomas Waring, was not in the same Gothic design as the Protestant chapels and was located adjacent to the portion of the cemetery allotted to the Roman Catholics. It had its own entrance from Pen-y-Wain Road, closer to Plucca Lane. The entrance from Allensbank Road had not yet been constructed. There are similarities between the details of the first floor windows of the Keeper's Lodge and those in the gable end of the chapel. However, as the original drawings show no porch or toilets, TW was asked in 1865 to design these. At the December meeting of 1865 these designs were accepted and he was instructed to advertise for tenders the following February, with Mr Shepton's tender of £118 being accepted.

As the cemetery had acquired 23 acres in 1879 and the portion of land allocated to the Roman Catholics was "being nearly all occupied" the officiating priest [possibly

Father Richardson] sent a letter to the Council requesting that their chapel be enlarged. This was discussed at the Committee Meeting on 18th August 1881 who ordered that a sub-committee consisting of three councillors (including Cllr Pat Carey) and the Borough Engineer inspect the building and report. A plan was drawn up which the committee recommended at the October meeting. The discussions then turned to providing a bell for the chapel and in 1884 plans were submitted for a belfry and bell and tenders were issued. The bell was made by Mr James Barwell of Birmingham for £36 8s 6d.

Entrance to Roman Catholic Chapel, circa 1905
Courtesy of Cardiff Capital Collection

Roman Catholic Chapel, 1890
Courtesy of Cardiff Capital Collection

This was not the end of the problems with the chapel, as the minutes of the committee show, that in 1888 such was the state of the chutes and glass of the chapel that the manager was instructed to have them repaired. In August 1889, whether or not it was to replace the original fittings, the dado around the chapel was "to be done at a cost not exceeding 30 shillings" and the font was "to be lined with lead at a cost not exceeding 10 shillings". The painting of the dado however was not done until the winter of 1890.

The Roman Catholic chapel, as can been seen in the illustration on the right, was not to survive to the 150th Anniversary and was demolished in 1986; close to the site of the chapel is the memorial to the Irish Famine disaster 1842-1849.

The Catholic Chapel prior to its demolition, 1986
Courtesy of Cardiff Capital Collection

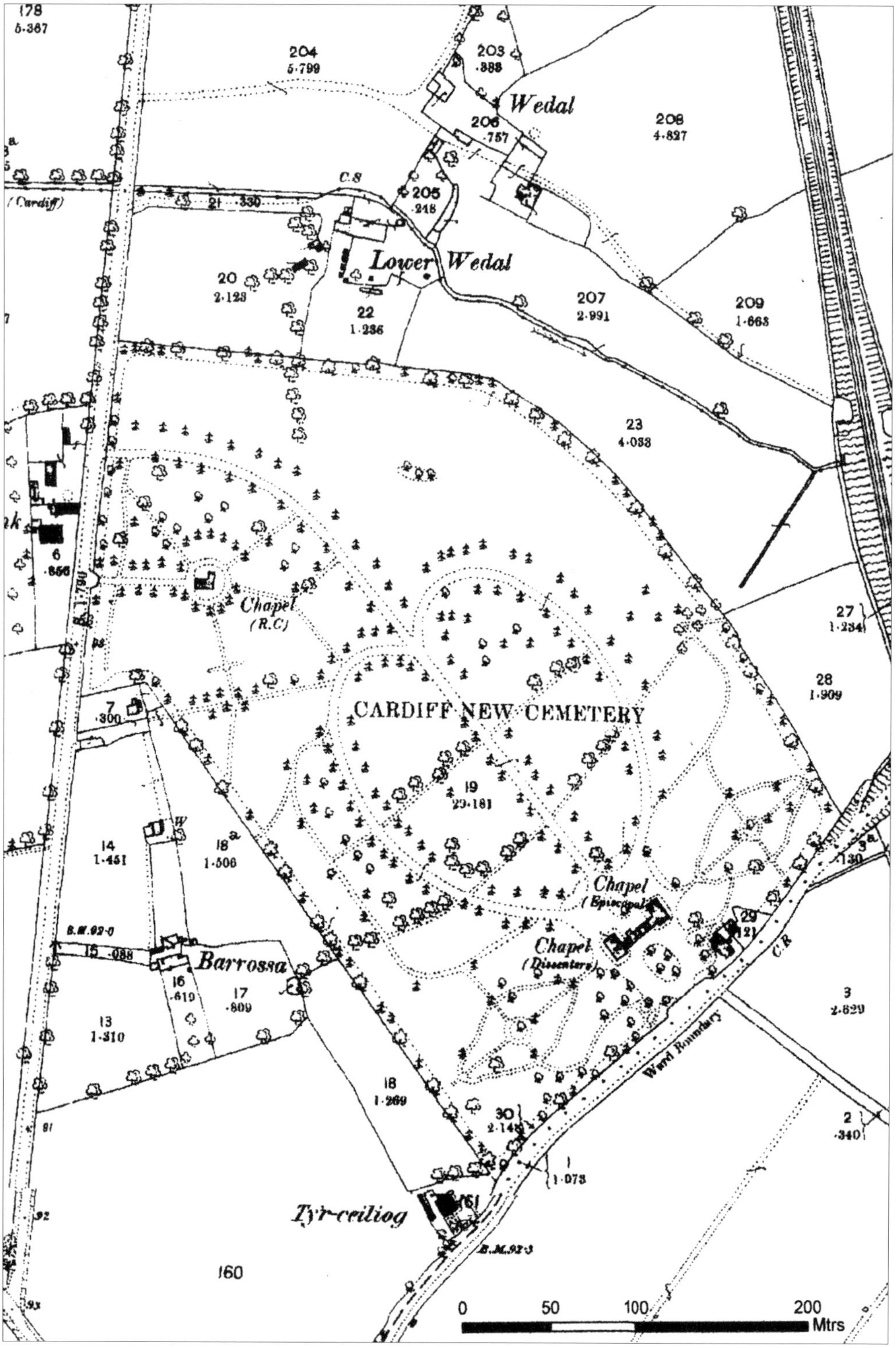

1887 Ordnance Survey Plan of Cemetery Area

Thomas Waring ceased to be the Surveyor/Architect in 1874 when his place was taken by a Mr T L Johnson who, in April 1876, was instructed to report on the best way to heat the chapels. At the meeting on 21st December 1876, a tender of £57 for heating the chapels [but not the vestries] from Mr Skinner of Stokes Croft, Bristol, was accepted.

As the years progressed the Borough Engineer was asked to report on the various problems that were affecting all of the chapels at one time or another. In August 1876 he was asked to report on the defective slates on the roofs of the chapels and in August 1878 the condition of the floor of the Catholic chapel was brought to his attention.

The boundary was originally of wooden fencing with thorn bushes on the inside to deter vandals and give some privacy, but they were soon found to be insufficient and costly to repair. In one or two areas the committee ordered that low brick walls be built. These measures, like the fences, were not that effective so more substantial boundary walls were required. In 1885 tenders from Mr James Allen of £2,191 for masonry and from Messrs Goddard and Marny of £588 for ironwork were accepted and the work started. The boundary now included the area of the Recreation Field and when visited in November 1885 the members of the committee were more than satisfied with the work. Work on the northern and eastern boundaries was to be undertaken as funds allowed into the 1890s. In the 1980s these walls were replaced in favour of a low wall with the wrought iron fences which we see today.

Nicholas Davey

CHAPTER THREE

History of the Cemetery – People, Problems and Plants

Organisation

Cardiff is fortunate that the minute books of the Cemetery Committee dated from 15th November 1860 to 20th September 1900 survive along with the Managers' reports and burial diaries and all are of great interest. It was not until a year after the opening that the Borough Council created a separate committee for the oversight of the running of the cemetery. So the surviving records enable the reader to understand how the cemetery was organised and evolved into its present state.

Cemetery Committee:

The Mayor	The ex-Mayor	Henry Bowen	Montague Grove	Richard H Mitchell
William Nell	George Smart	John Thomas	John Winstone	

Montague Grove was appointed Chairman at the first meeting on 15th November 1860 and it was decided that their meetings would be held on the Thursday prior to the quarterly meetings of the Burial Board. [The Burial Board meetings were held after each of the full council meetings until 1879 when they were separated from the main council meetings.]

At the second meeting on 27th November 1860 it was resolved that "an analysis of the burials and of the receipts and payments were to be submitted to the committee at each meeting".

Every design for headstones and monuments was to be scrutinised by the committee and only what was on the drawing [including kerb stones] was allowed. The graves were all to be marked by cast iron or later slate crosses [no wooden ones were allowed in the cemetery] and their requisition and cost feature in many of the committee meetings.

Fees

One problem that exercised the minds of the committee members was that the cemetery had to pay its way and it was calculated that the employees and maintenance costs would be about £320 per annum, in addition to repayment of the £12,000 purchase price [with interest]. It was estimated that, if there were 600 burials each year at an average cost of 10 shillings, they would only bring in £300 per annum so the cemetery would not be self-supporting for the first year or two.

The Council set the burial fees prior to November 1860 so it was not until the committee meeting of 11th May 1863 that they were discussed again, and any alteration to the fees was deferred until the next meeting, on 18th June 1863, when the new fees and rules were adopted.

In 1865 William Timms wrote to the committee about these fees and explained that they only covered two classes of burials – Pauper and First Class. He suggested the adoption of a Middle Class, at half-price extra – viz. 5 shillings, as many of the bereaved families would prefer to pay more rather than have their loved ones buried as Paupers.

It is not recorded if the suggestion was taken up then but by 1914 the fees have three rates, Vault, Ordinary Grave and Pauper.

At their meeting on 17th September 1863, the committee discussed a letter from a Mr Hodkinson asking upon what terms the parishioners of Roath could be buried at the Cardiff Cemetery. The recommendation was that the Table of Fees be sent with a letter explaining why non-parishioners of Cardiff are charged more than parishioners.

This difference in fees would remain until 1875 when the city boundaries were extended to include the parish of Roath and Splott, Grangetown and Canton in the parish of Llandaff.

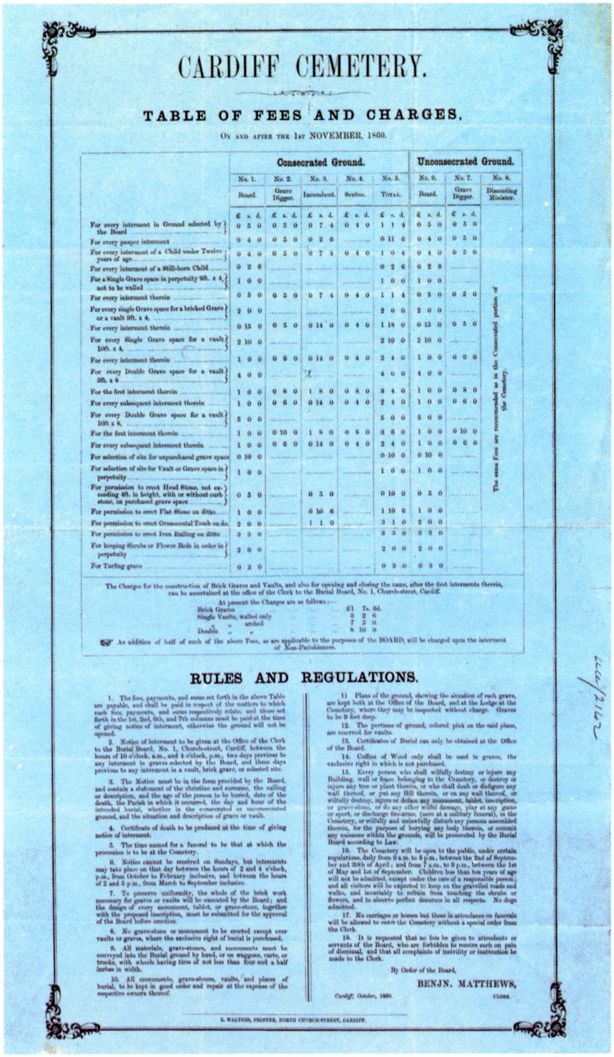

CARDIFF CEMETERY.

TABLE OF FEES AND CHARGES,

ON AND AFTER THE 1ST NOVEMBER, 1860.

	Consecrated Ground.					Unconsecrated Ground.		
	No. 1. Board.	No. 2. Grave Digger.	No. 3. Incumbent.	No. 4. Sexton.	No. 5. TOTAL.	No. 6. Board.	No. 7. Grave Digger.	No. 8. Dissenting Minister.
	£ s. d.	£ s. d.	£ s. d.	£ s. d.	£ s. d.	£ s. d.	£ s. d.	
For every interment in Ground selected by the Board	0 5 0	0 5 0	0 7 4	0 4 0	1 1 4	0 5 0	0 5 0	The same Fees are recommended as in the Consecrated portion of the Cemetery.
For every pauper interment	0 4 0	0 5 0	0 2 6		0 11 6	0 4 0	0 5 0	
For every interment of a Child under Twelve years of age	0 4 0	0 5 0	0 7 4	0 4 0	1 0 4	0 4 0	0 5 0	
For every interment of a Still-born Child	0 2 6				0 2 6	0 2 6		
For a Single Grave space in perpetuity 9ft. x 4, not to be walled	1 0 0				1 0 0	1 0 0		
For every interment therein	0 5 0	0 5 0	0 7 4	0 4 0	1 1 4	0 5 0	0 5 0	
For every single Grave space for a bricked Grave or a vault 9ft. x 4,	2 0 0				2 0 0	2 0 0		
For every interment therein	0 15 0	0 5 0	0 14 0	0 4 0	1 18 0	0 15 0	0 5 0	
For every Single Grave space for a vault 10ft. x 4,	2 10 0				2 10 0	2 10 0		
For every interment therein	1 0 0	0 6 0	0 14 0	0 4 0	2 4 0	1 0 0	0 6 0	
For every Double Grave space for a vault 9ft. x 8	4 0 0				4 0 0	4 0 0		
For the first interment therein	1 0 0	0 8 0	1 8 0	0 8 0	3 4 0	1 0 0	0 8 0	
For every subsequent interment therein	1 0 0	0 6 0	0 14 0	0 4 0	2 4 0	1 0 0	0 6 0	
For every Double Grave space for a vault 10ft x 8,	5 0 0				5 0 0	5 0 0		
For the first interment therein	1 0 0	0 10 0	1 8 0	0 8 0	3 6 0	1 0 0	0 10 0	
For every subsequent interment therein	1 0 0	0 6 0	0 14 0	0 4 0	2 4 0	1 0 0	0 6 0	
For selection of site for unpurchased grave space	0 10 0				0 10 0	0 10 0		
For selection of site for Vault or Grave space in perpetuity	1 0 0				1 0 0	1 0 0		
For permission to erect Head Stone, not exceeding 4ft. in height, with or without curb stone, on purchased grave space	0 5 0		0 5 0		0 10 0	0 5 0		
For permission to erect Flat Stone on ditto	1 0 0		0 10 6		1 10 6	1 0 0		
For permission to erect Ornamental Tomb on do.	2 0 0		1 1 0		3 1 0	2 0 0		
For permission to erect Iron Railing on ditto	3 3 0				3 3 0	3 3 0		
For keeping Shrubs or Flower Beds in order in perpetuity	2 0 0				2 0 0	2 0 0		
For Turfing grave	0 3 0				0 3 0	0 3 0		

The Charges for the construction of Brick Graves and Vaults, and also for opening and closing the same, after the first interments therein, can be ascertained at the office of the Clerk to the Burial Board, No. 1, Church-street, Cardiff.

At present the Charges are as follows:—

Brick Graves	£1	7s.	8d.
Single Vaults, walled only	3	2	6
" " arched	7	5	0
Double " "	8	10	0

☞ An addition of half of each of the above Fees, as are applicable to the purposes of the BOARD, will be charged upon the interment of Non-Parishioners.

RULES AND REGULATIONS.

1. The fees, payments, and sums set forth in the above Table are payable, and shall be paid in respect of the matters to which such fees, payments, and sums respectively relate, and those set forth in the 1st, 2nd, 6th, and 7th columns must be paid at the time of giving notice of interment, otherwise the ground will not be opened.

2. Notice of interment to be given at the Office of the Clerk to the Burial Board, No. 1, Church-street, Cardiff, between the hours of 10 o'clock, a.m., and 4 o'clock, p.m., two days previous to any interment in graves selected by the Board, and three days previous to any interment in a vault, brick grave, or selected site.

3. The Notice must be in the form provided by the Board, and contain a statement of the christian and surname, the calling or description, and the age of the person to be buried, date of the death, the Parish in which it occurred, the day and hour of the intended burial, whether in the consecrated or unconsecrated ground, and the situation and description of grave or vault.

4. Certificate of death to be produced at the time of giving notice of interment.

5. The time named for a funeral to be that at which the procession is to be at the Cemetery.

6. Notice cannot be received on Sundays, but interments may take place on that day between the hours of 2 and 4 o'clock, p.m., from October to February inclusive, and between the hours of 2 and 5 p.m., from March to September inclusive.

7. To preserve uniformity, the whole of the brick work necessary for graves or vaults will be executed by the Board; and the design of every monument, tablet, or grave-stone, together with the proposed inscription, must be submitted for the approval of the Board before erection.

8. No grave-stone or monument to be erected except over vaults or graves, where the exclusive right of burial is purchased.

9. All materials, grave-stones, and monuments must be conveyed into the Burial ground by hand, or on waggons, carts, or trucks, with wheels having tires of not less than four and a half inches in width.

10. All monuments, grave-stones, vaults, and places of burial, to be kept in good order and repair at the expense of the respective owners thereof.

11. Plans of the ground, showing the situation of each grave, are kept both at the Office of the Board, and at the Lodge at the Cemetery, where they may be inspected without charge. Graves to be 9 feet deep.

12. The portions of ground, colored pink on the said plans, are reserved for vaults.

13. Certificates of Burial can only be obtained at the Office of the Board.

14. Coffins of Wood only shall be used in graves, the exclusive right in which is not purchased.

15. Every person who shall wilfully destroy or injure any Building, wall or fence belonging to the Cemetery, or destroy or injure any tree or plant therein, or who shall daub or disfigure any wall thereof, or put any Bill therein, or on any wall thereof, or wilfully destroy, injure or deface any monument, tablet, inscription, or grave-stone, or do any other wilful damage, play at any game or sport, or discharge fire-arms, (save at a military funeral), in the Cemetery, or wilfully and unlawfully disturb any persons assembled therein, for the purpose of burying any body therein, or commit any nuisance within the grounds, will be prosecuted by the Burial Board according to Law.

16. The Cemetery will be open to the public, under certain regulations, daily from 9 a.m. to 5 p.m., between the 2nd of September and 30th of April; and from 7 a.m., to 9 p.m., between the 1st of May and 1st of September. Children less than ten years of age will not be admitted, except under the care of a responsible person; and all visitors will be expected to keep on the gravelled roads and walks, and invariably to refrain from touching the shrubs or flowers, and to observe perfect decorum in all respects. No dogs admitted.

17. No carriages or horses but those in attendance on funerals will be allowed to enter the Cemetery without a special order from the Clerk.

18. It is requested that no fees be given to attendants or servants of the Board, who are forbidden to receive such on pain of dismissal, and that all complaints of incivility or inattention be made to the Clerk.

By Order of the Board,

BENJN. MATTHEWS,

Cardiff, October, 1860. CLERK.

E. WALTERS, PRINTER, NORTH CHURCH-STREET, CARDIFF.

Charges and Regulations from 1861

By permission of Llyfrgell Genedlaethol Cymru /The National Library of Wales

Hours

Burials took place Sunday to Saturday between 9am and 2pm but in 1871 the Clerk to the committee wrote to various Burial Boards of the larger towns in England and Wales on the subject of Burials on Sunday. Various views on the subject were obtained from these towns and the Government. Also, following a "Memorial" from the Rev'd Blanchflower and other Nonconformist ministers requesting that the practice cease except in the case of emergency, the committee decided that the practice should cease from 1st May 1873.

In September 1881 the committee standardised the times of burials as:

- 1st March to 30th September 10am to 5pm
- 1st October to 28th February 10am to 4pm.

Problems

Almost as soon as the cemetery was opened the first major problem was discovered with the drainage. Although the Surveyor had dug six trial pits to ascertain the water level of the site it was not until November [by which time the weather had changed] that those pits showed that the site was prone to flooding. He then reported to the Burial Board that he had dug a total of twenty pits and they were now overflowing. The Surveyor and R G Thomas had held discussions about the problem and they estimated that the costs of drainage would be £1800. The point that exercised both the Burial Board and the reporter of *The Cardiff Times* was that the highest ground was the wettest. The decision was left to the Board of Health since there were two options, drainage through the Cathays Sewer or through the Roath Brook.

Following the decision of the Board of Health an estimate was obtained from the Architect and the Engineer which was deemed excessive, so members of the Cemetery Committee visited the site with "skilled men" and subsequently it was decided on 7th November 1861, that the high ground be drained through the existing pipework which runs into the Cathays Sewer. On 23rd December 1861, tenders were advertised for the drain. Mr James Turner's tender of £48 was accepted, as the cheapest, on 6th February 1862 but he was paid £43 on 12th May 1862.

The drainage was to be a problem for the further landscaping and hard planting in the following years. In February 1868 the Manager reported that there was a quantity of water in the graves when they were opened.

Although the boundaries were fixed in 1859, in May 1874 the ditch and fence that formed the boundary with Little Wedal Farm was encroached upon by Mr Moore, the occupier of the farm. This was still a problem in September 1874 when the Town Clerk was requested to take further action.

Trespassers and thefts of flowers etc were such a problem that the committee allowed the manager to deal with them. In some cases he did not report the people to the magistrates but in November 1877 he was instructed to ask the Town Clerk to prosecute George Sutton of Letty Street, Cathays for removing stones from the cemetery heap. The Surveyor was instructed to use the remainder of the stones for highway purposes.

A certain David John Rees of 69 Merthyr Street was prosecuted and convicted on the 8th June 1894 under the Burial Causes Act of 1847 for plucking a rose in the cemetery on Sunday 3rd June. A fine of 40s and costs was imposed, so as with all criminal acts they were taken very seriously at the time.

By June 1878 some of the monuments were in a dilapidated condition and the Town Clerk was instructed to write to the owners concerned requiring either their removal or replacement in a better state of repair.

Employees

In 1859 when the cemetery was opened it was to be maintained by a Head Gardener and a small team of grave diggers.

The Cardiff Times of 12th November 1859 has the following to say about the appointment of Henry Timms, the first Head Gardener :

Cardiff Burial Board
Meeting to elect the Gardener
Candidates:-

Farrell from Bristol, Tims [sic] from Canton, Richins from Gloucester, Large from Neath, Thomas from Merthyr and Wallbridge from Cardiff.

A variety of questions were asked and testimonials were given and when it had all been gone through Mr Watkins rose to propose Mr Tims as a fit and proper person. For the last thirty years Mr Tims had been resident in this town and neighbourhood and had embarked a large capital in the cultivation of trees. In fact in this trade he was before his day and consequently lost a great deal of money as a nurseryman. He was a very industrious man and his wife a very industrious woman. No man was more competent for the office and he thought as an old inhabitant they would do well to appoint him.

Alderman Vachell proposed Mr T Thomas
Mr H Bird proposed Mr Ritchins
Alderman Morgan Mr Large.
At the final vote Mr Tims was duly elected.

William Henry Timms, a native of Coventry, who in 1844 lived and worked from Cathays Nursery, which was located next to Cathays Park, [then the pleasure gardens of Cardiff Castle] before the castle grounds were developed by Andrew Pettigrew. They are now the site of the Cardiff University.

Mr Timms' wages were set at "£1 per week with house and coals included". Living in the Lodge, the gardener was responsible for completion of the register of the burials, for keeping the grounds in proper order and superintending the digging of the graves.

Two sextons employed under the gardener, whose fees for digging graves in consecrated ground were originally 3s for an ordinary funeral and 7s for a vault. The space allotted for vaults was to be 10ft by 4ft and the charge for constructing a vault was set at £11. However, after some discussion with the Bishop and Rev Canon Morgan, the sextons' fees were set at 5s for digging graves in consecrated ground. These two sextons were augmented by an additional man in August 1861. By May 1862 the cemetery required another two men for the months of May to July.

A clerk was employed to undertake the registration of burials and record other legal charges that would have to be made independently, such as searching the register and making out certificates etc. The Town Clerk suggested that for searching the register for one year the charge would be 1s and for every year afterwards sixpence. A certified copy of the register would cost 2s 6d and for making out the title to a piece of freehold in the burial ground 3s 6d. The first clerk, Mr Matthews, had been undertaking the registration of burials prior to the official opening of cemetery in October 1859 and he continued for a few months until Mr E P Richards was appointed.

As the cemetery was getting busy the paths and drives were being damaged and on 11th May 1863 Mr Timms suggested that women should be employed to undertake the task of sweeping them. The committee agreed with this and four women were employed. However their wages were not to be more than that which had been paid the previous year. This policy was to continue for many years.

As the graves were dug a considerable amount of stone was uncovered and discarded but had to be removed from the cemetery. In May 1861 the committee decided to sell the stone at 7d a load however the buyers had to collect it themselves. At the same time it was decided that a donkey and cart should be purchased for use within the cemetery; this is not to be confused with the hand-drawn bier that the committee purchased in 1860 and housed in the bier-house next to the mortuary chapels.

After Mr Timms' death in 1867 a new Manager and Lodge Keeper was appointed, but the minute books do not name him. Mr Timms was buried in the cemetery that he had cared for and developed from rough pasture to landscaped parkland.

Grave of William Timms
Nicholas Davy

Numbers and Visitors

The Manager would report to the monthly committee meeting the statistics of the burials that had taken place in the previous month. These were divided between the Non-consecrated, Consecrated and Roman Catholic burials and then by age groups within each parish that the Burial Board administered.

Within the report he was also able to make comments about various events that occurred in the Cemetery as follows:

> *Palm Sunday April 1904*
> *Upwards of 100,000 visitors passed through the cemetery during the day and glad to say not a single case of pilfering or complaint reported.*

This is the first mention in any of the surviving records of the Tradition of *Sul yr Bledau* which took place on Palm Sunday. It involved visiting family graves and apart from cleaning them, they would be decorated with spring flowers, such as daffodils, and herbs.

The number of visitors in April 1904 could well have been the result of the revival of religion that had started in Wales in the early months of the year.

One of the marks of the revival was the general effect of good behaviour within the entire population, as can be seen on Palm Sunday 1905, when many thousands of visitors passed through the cemetery during the day, and the Manager was again "glad to say not a single case of pilfering or complaint reported".

From 23rd March 1908 the monthly report is compiled by Mr C Willis who takes the opportunity to write at length all of his complaints about the running of the cemetery. For example this is how he reports the Palm Sunday celebrations in April 1908:

"many thousands of visitors. Should be glad in future of some police on duty in Cemetery."

On 22nd June 1908 his report covers 2 pages on various topics ranging from an exhumation and problems with the cemetery horse to a problem of fly-tipping.

In April 1909 the Manager not only had Palm Sunday celebrations, which got out of hand, to cope with but on the following Monday afternoon the Chinese population of Cardiff visited the graves of their ancestors with offerings of fruit, sweets, oranges and a whole roast pig. "The Chinese left to themselves would have caused no damage ... it was the onlookers who caused the damage with their pushing and jostling."

Mr Willis was not always complaining but had some good suggestions such as giving relatives at a burial a slip of paper with the plot number and location and also the opening times of the cemetery to help them relocate a grave without disturbing the Manager or his wife. In 1909 he also asked for advice about burials in the ground near the library facing Gladstone School, as they would shortly commence burials there.

Palm Sunday 1891
Courtesy of Cardiff Capital Collection

Landscaping

The Cemetery was landscaped in the current style of the time as a park with flowerbeds, shrubs and trees, as can be seen in the picture opposite, and as *The Cardiff Times* reported at the time "we have no doubt that in a short time, not only will the cemetery have a pretty appearance but that it will form the principal walk of the inhabitants of the town of Cardiff...." At the time of the opening of the cemetery there was no park for the uninterrupted use of the population of the Borough of Cardiff. You could, by ticket, enter Coopers Field behind Cardiff Castle on a Sunday afternoon. It was patrolled by staff of the Bute Estate who could expel people who misbehaved or were not in favour with the

A view of the Cemetery dated 1870, but probably later
Courtesy of Cardiff Capital Collection

family. There is a famous incident involving the wife of John Bachelor, who during the time of her husband's year as Mayor was refused admission to the Castle Grounds because he was a political opponent of the Bute family.

The design centred on a heart shape with the apex of its paths just inside the arched entrance on the south east edge of the cemetery. The two Chapels and the Lodge were situated at this point while to the north west near the path, the Roman Catholic chapel was situated. It is smaller than the others but similar in character adjoining the portion of the ground allotted for Catholic burials and had been provided with a gate for their especial use.

Planting

We know from the newspaper accounts who first planted the cemetery but it is not clear if it was his design.

> *"The central drive has an avenue of horse-chestnut trees, and forms the boundary between the consecrated and unconsecrated portions of the ground; after dividing the ground it terminates in a separate entrance from Plucca Lane. The whole of the grounds have been well stocked with trees and shrubs, and flower beds having been formed opposite the chapels, and around the keeper's lodge. This part of the contract was performed by Mr Matthews of the Cardiff nursery".*

However, as a report from Mr Timms on 12th August 1861 to the Cemetery Committee recommended that 600 scotch and spruce be purchased, this suggests that some of the areas of the cemetery were without hard planting. The Committee also authorised bills for grass seed from J B Hopkins to be paid. The trees were brought from a Mr J S Matthews and he was paid £8 for them some time around 19th June 1862.

Mr Timms had experience in designing the planting having been for several years the owner of the Cathays Nursery as can be seen in the Catalogue printed in the 1830's and illustrated on page 25.

At the February Meeting in 1862 it was resolved to purchase 1000 Thorn quicks, probably of the Hawthorn family such as Blackthorn, Whitethorn and May tree, to be used as hedging to mark the boundaries of the cemetery; it appears that these cost £8 from J S Matthews. The boundaries were defined by a fence along Fairoak Road and in 1868 quicks were planted alongside it.

On 22nd December 1862 Mr Timms was allowed to prepare 6 beds on either side of the entrance for flowers and shrubs. He reported to the Cemetery Committee that 50 shrubs would be required in March or April as 50 of the 600 firs that had previously been planted had failed. This failure he attributed to want of stakes that were strong enough to stand the extremes of weather that the position of the cemetery had to bear. Where the digging of the drainage ditch had taken place it would require another 100 shrubs and to keep the grass green 50 sacks of soot and 5 pounds of Dutch clover. These shrubs were brought from Treseders at the cost of £5 for Shrubs and Mr Hopkins was paid 3s 6d for seeds on 11th May 1863.

In November 1864 100 Spruce fir trees and 200 Yew trees were purchased from

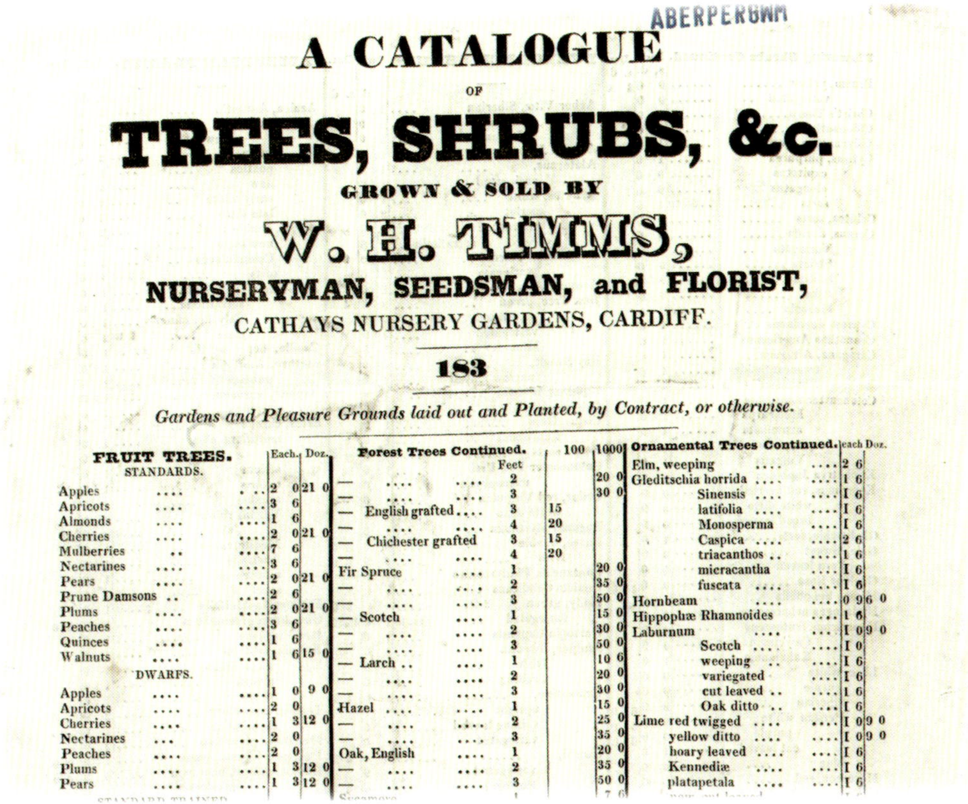

ABERPERGWM

A CATALOGUE

OF

TREES, SHRUBS, &c.

GROWN & SOLD BY

W. H. TIMMS,

NURSERYMAN, SEEDSMAN, and FLORIST,

CATHAYS NURSERY GARDENS, CARDIFF.

183

Gardens and Pleasure Grounds laid out and Planted, by Contract, or otherwise.

FRUIT TREES.	Each.	Doz.
STANDARDS.		
Apples	2 0	21 0
Apricots	3 6	
Almonds	1 6	
Cherries	2 0	21 0
Mulberries ..	7 6	
Nectarines	3 6	
Pears	2 0	21 0
Prune Damsons ..	2 6	
Plums	2 0	21 0
Peaches	3 6	
Quinces	1 6	
Walnuts	1 6	15 0
DWARFS.		
Apples	1 0	9 0
Apricots	2 0	
Cherries	1 3	12 0
Nectarines ...	2 0	
Peaches	2 0	
Plums	1 3	12 0
Pears	1 3	12 0

Forest Trees Continued.	Feet	100	1000
—	2		20 0
—	3		30 0
— English grafted	3	15	
—	4	20	
— Chichester grafted	3	15	
—	4	20	
Fir Spruce	1		20 0
—	2		35 0
—	3		50 0
— Scotch	1		15 0
—	2		30 0
—	3		50 0
— Larch	1		10 6
—	2		20 0
—	3		30 0
Hazel	1		15 0
—	2		25 0
—	3		35 0
Oak, English	1		20 0
—	2		35 0
—	3		50 0

Ornamental Trees Continued.	each	Doz.
Elm, weeping	2 6	
Gleditschia horrida	1 6	
Sinensis	I 6	
latifolia	I 6	
Monosperma	I 6	
Caspica	2 6	
triacanthos ..	1 6	
micracantha	I 6	
fuscata	I 6	
Hornbeam	0 9	6 0
Hippophæ Rhamnoides	1 6	
Laburnum	I 0	9 0
Scotch	I 0	
weeping ..	I 6	
variegated	I 6	
cut leaved ..	1 6	
Oak ditto ..	I 6	
Lime red twigged	I 0	9 0
yellow ditto	I 0	9 0
hoary leaved	I 6	
Kennediæ	I 6	
platapetala	I 6	

Extract from Mr Timms' Catalogue
By permission of Llyfrgell Genedlaethol Cymru / The National Library of Wales

Treseders, at a cost of £4 15s, to fill up vacant spaces in the cemetery ground; this was caused by continued failure of the previous planting to have taken.

Following the Committee Meeting on 8th February 1866 the cemetery was planted with 75 Yews, 25 Laurels, 10 Red Cedars, 25 Portugal Laurels, 10 Rhododendrons, 25 Laurestina/Laurestine to replace the failures, and 44 shrubs of different sorts for the two new beds at the back of the chapels. These plants were all obtained from William Treseders for £10 10s 3d.

Mr Timms' last request for shrubs was made on 21st March 1867 and was as follows : 50 Laurel, 50 Larch, 25 Laurestones/ Laurestines, 10 Arbor Nitae/ Arbor-Vitae, 25 Portugal Laurel, 12 Aucuba Japoniea/ Aucuba Japonica, 10 Arbulus Unedo and 2 Variegated Holly. Again these were obtained from William Treseder for £4 10s 0d.

During his time as Manager of the cemetery Mr Timms had problems not only from visitors, planting failures and drains but animals appear to have caused him a few problems as the minutes contain entries for payments to Mole Catchers. At the Committee Meeting on 19th March 1863 Mr Bond, whose land adjoined the cemetery where he had pigs, threatened legal action as his pigs had been impounded for trespassing at the cemetery. This land was supposed to have been walled in by a dwarf wall following the Meeting of the 20th March 1862.

The new manager did not request particular shrubs or plants but was allowed various amounts ranging from £3 in November 1867, £6.12s.6d in June 1868, £10 in November 1868, £5 in November 1869 and £1.10s in November 1870. There are no exact details of what plants were purchased but from the amounts paid to various nurserymen they included:

1867	*November*	*Bulbs*
1868	*March*	*Hardy Annuals and other plants*
	June	*J S Matthews for Quicks (Thorns), Annuals and Shrubs*
1869	*September*	*Shrubs from J S Matthews*
	November	*500 Strong Thorn Quicks*
1870	*March*	*Hardy Annuals and other plants*
	June	*One bushel of mixed Grass seed*
	August	*Shrubs purchased from William Treseder*
		Bulbs from William Treseder.

So these later purchases suggest that the majority of the trees and shrubs that had been planted by Timms were surviving and his planting scheme was being preserved with only a few shrubs being replaced and annual bedding and winter or spring bulbs being planted.

This plan for replacement and annual planting continued for many years and the only alteration to the original design was in 1889 when the Committee resolved to have the flower beds in front of the chapels facing Fairoak Road reduced in size and planted with annual flowers. This was changed in October 1889 to shrubs; obviously the bedding plants did not meet with the Committee's approval and would be cheaper.

Due to the cost of purchasing bedding plants it was suggested in September 1889 that a greenhouse be erected. This had not taken place before because William Treseder had been granted the contract but in June 1908 the Manager questioned this policy and suggested that a greenhouse would enable the bedding plants to be grown at a far cheaper cost. However the suggestion did not meet with the Committee's approval.

As the years progressed the original planting of trees and shrubs outgrew the design so they were removed along with wind-sown trees such as willows and laurels, much the same as today when working parties from the Council or the Friends group undertake this clearance.

Nicholas Davey

CHAPTER FOUR

Today and Tomorrow

Large Victorian cemeteries such as Cathays are expensive to maintain. Cutting the grass alone costs tens of thousand of pounds each year. On the other hand, the old part of the cemetery is, in practical terms, full, so its original role as a place of interment has virtually ceased and this means that there is no income to support maintenance. Inevitably, a balance has to be drawn between respect for those buried there and their families, the benefits to today's community and the cost of maintaining the cemetery.

Look around and you will see evidence of how this balance has been exercised in the past. In the 1970s, memorials in some sections were moved from their original position and placed back to back in rows without any kerb sets. This creates space for large machines to cut the grass, saving on labour costs. This process of lawn conversion does, however, change the character of the cemetery. Since the 1980s only those memorials that are dilapidated or present a danger to visitors are moved. All other memorials are left in situ, thus preserving them for future generations to enjoy and learn from. In some of the oldest parts of the cemetery, lack of active maintenance resulted in trees, large shrubs and brambles taking hold and making some memorials inaccessible. Works have been carried out in the last few years, including workdays by the Friends of Cathays Cemetery, to address this problem.

Tackling shrubbery on Friends workday
John Farnhill

Relative newcomers to the area may not be aware that the original boundary railings were removed during the Second World War to be melted down for munitions. But the site has been refurbished and new railings installed to recreate some of the cemetery's Victorian splendour.

What this illustrates is that different generations will have different priorities and will interpret the criteria for maintaining a balance between benefit and cost in different ways. It is likely that some of the decisions made in the past would be frowned upon today, that it will not be possible to get unanimous support for everything that we do today and that future generations will think that we made mistakes and will endeavour to compensate for them.

Green space to be enjoyed
Bereavement Services

In Victorian times cemeteries were laid out as places of education as well as places for the burial of the dead. As green spaces open to the public, they were to be places to be enjoyed and were laid out in much the same way as a park. If these were wise principles when burials were taking place, they are even more important now. So what is being done to ensure that these ideals flourish and to prevent the cemetery becoming a neglected white elephant?

Area in need of clearance
John Farnhill

In 2002 a conservation policy was established for Cathays Cemetery. The idea was to create and preserve a natural habitat for wildlife within an urban cemetery environment and enable natural plants and flowers to flourish. The policy leaves five large sections within the oldest part of the cemetery as conservation areas, which are identified by notices. Where families require access to graves a path will be cut to that particular grave and maintained throughout the season. Otherwise, the grass is cut once a year at the end of the autumn while other works, such as cutting back brambles from memorials and clearing overgrown pathways, will generally be programmed for the winter months. It is particularly important that this work takes due account of wildlife so, for example, cutting back natural growth does not take place during the nesting season.

Wild flowers from targeted sowing
Bereavement Services

Today, the cemetery presents a variety of landscapes which support a wide variety of insects, birds and animals. In keeping with Victorian ideals the cemetery was laid out with evergreen trees, with its central area designed in a symmetrical way. Later, native deciduous trees were planted and there has been some natural regeneration. This latter includes the spread of wild flowers, such as primrose, wood anemone, celandine and bluebell, which put on a magnificent display in the spring. This has been enhanced in recent years by targeted sowing of wildflower seeds in two discrete areas to add to the visual experience for those visiting and using the cemetery.

As the third largest Victorian Cemetery in the United Kingdom, Cathays has tremendous heritage value. It is the final resting place of most of the people who guided the city through its hectic development during the 19th and early 20th centuries, so many of the memorials have a tale to tell – as we shall see later in this book. These same memorials provide an exhibition of the symbolism traditionally used. Many of the symbols derive from the classical world of the Greeks and Romans, such as the draped urn, the victor's wreath and the broken column. Other examples include a tree standing on a rock indicating a strong attachment to religion, a cut in a bough representing a life cut off in its prime, an upturned torch as a further symbol of a life extinguished and an anchor epitomising hope for the life beyond death. Perhaps more poignantly, ivy growing up a bough is a symbol of immortality and the artistry of such memorials helps to ensure for the deceased a degree of immortality.

Example of Victorian memorial symbolism
Gordon Hindess

It will be clear from the above that the cemetery does indeed represent a significant educational resource and this is being presented in a number of ways. Work has been carried out using the Living Churchyard project, which allows primary schools to use the cemetery as an educational resource, looking at the history of the site and the community it has served over the last 150 years, as well as examining some of the habitats for wildlife, wildflowers and insects. This project is supported by the 'Hunt the Daisy' pack which includes work-sheets and information for teachers and pupils at Key Stages 1 and 2, ranging from maths topics to mini beast surveys. The Living Churchyard promotes the principles and practices of nature conservation within cemeteries and churchyards.

The cemetery has been used for work at Geography GCSE level and by the University for geology studies. Work is currently being carried out with Careers Wales to introduce primary and secondary schools to the Cathays Cemetery as an educational resource.

For a less formal approach to the educational aspects of the cemetery, three Trail Guides have been produced. The Heritage Trail looks at the heritage of Cathays Cemetery from the founding fathers of Cardiff buried in the cemetery to the pauper 'balloon girl' Louisa Maud Evans. The Insignia Trail considers the Commonwealth War Graves Commission headstones placed throughout Cathays Cemetery. Each regiment is considered through the walk looking at the regimental insignia and any interesting facts such as the 'nickname' of a particular regiment. The impact of World War II on the cemetery is also considered. The Tree Trail, as you might expect, looks at the trees planted in the cemetery, which contains many fine species such as the Cedar of Lebanon and the Monkey Puzzle.

Throughout the year, it is possible to join an open guided walk, while these may also be arranged especially for individual groups. Talks can also be arranged to suit the requirements of particular groups. For casual visitors, there is normally a member of the staff of Bereavement Services on site who will be pleased to assist, whether it be to answer a general enquiry or a quest for a particular grave.

One of the popular guided walks
John Farnhill

Perhaps the most important single resource in the cemetery is the chapel building, although this may not be too obvious from its current neglected condition. As we have seen in an earlier chapter, the chapels are of historic importance, but they have been listed by CADW as 'buildings at risk'. As the 150th anniversary approaches, it is pleasing to see a start being made on the restoration of the chapels with the restoration of the roof structure. It is hoped that this will enable the fencing to be removed from around the outside making them more accessible to the public. Further interim improvements may also see the replacement of the wooden panels in the windows with Plexiglas, allowing more light into the buildings and improving the general appearance of the chapels. There are no utility services in the chapels and these will also have to be looked at if they are to be brought back into use.

The key to funding the restoration of the chapels is to find a sustainable use for them. Some of the options looked at have included using the chapels as a heritage centre, workshop or for a small business which is in keeping with the situation. At the time of writing, exploratory discussions are underway to see if one of the chapels could be used as both a burial chapel and as a community resource with educational and meeting space accommodated within the building.

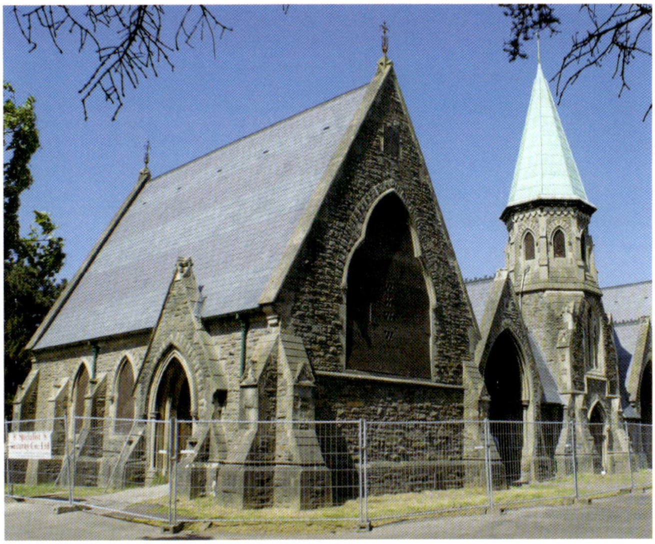

Chapel roof just after re-slating, May 2009
Tony Price

Looking to the future, there is a Regeneration Plan for the cemetery which aims to establish a long term strategy with funding to build on the good work of recent years. It should not be expected that an instant transformation will take place, but the underlying objective will be to secure what already exists, promote progressive improvement and look for opportunities within what, in the short term at least, is expected to be a period of financial stringency. Re-use of the chapels and increasing visitor numbers would require improved permanent toilet facilities.

With increasing interest in genealogical research, the transfer of all old paper records into a digital archive and the establishment of a genealogical research facility have been suggested. If people were looking for the grave of an ancestor, then section marker posts and key plans at the main entrances would make this much easier. As visitor numbers increase, more seats might be appreciated. It is apparent that the re-discovery of memorials as a result of clearance work and research by various individuals is producing further interesting information about people and events that could enhance the existing trails (or provide additional ones) or support the publication of further books.

What is certain is that things cannot stand still. Maintenance and restoration of the cemetery depends on increasing use being made of this valuable heritage and environmental resource but, hopefully, it may once again form the 'principal walk for the people of Cardiff' envisaged by its Victorian founders. It is likely that our children will come up with innovative ideas to put Cathays Cemetery to beneficial use. As an example of how changing times can introduce new possibilities, the remainder of the chapter explains how a game that could not have been anticipated at the end of the 20th century is now bringing visitors to the cemetery … and recording their appreciation of the experience.

Cathays Cemetery Geocache – the 21st century way to explore this Victorian treasure

A geocache is part of a worldwide game dedicated to GPS (Global Positioning System) users, called Geocaching. The game involves a GPS user hiding a container holding "treasure" and publishing its coordinates so other GPS users can go on a "treasure hunt" to find it. The only rules are: if you take something from the cache, you must leave something of similar value in return, and you must write about your visit in the logbook in the cache. You should also log your visit online at the cache website, thus providing a digital record of activity at the cache.

It is truly a 21st century game. In May 2000, the United States government officially removed selective availability from their GPS satellites, enabling civilian GPS units to have greater accuracy than previously allowed. Within days, an enthusiast had hidden a container in the Oregon countryside and posted the coordinates on the Internet, inviting others to find it. Geocaching sprang from this one simple posting and its growth has been phenomenal. By 2008, geocaching was active in more than 200 countries and there were more than 30,000 caches in the UK, with in excess of 1000 in Wales.

Several variations of the game have evolved. Micro- and nano-caches are used to overcome the challenge of hiding them in urban locations: a typical micro-cache might use a 35mm film canister, while a nano-cache might be no bigger than a sugar cube! The coordinates for an offset cache will take you to a location where you must find more information and apply your wits in order to get to the final cache container. The logical extension to this is the multicache, where you must visit several locations in order to get to the container: these can be very useful if the aim is to provide a guided tour to an area. All of these can be turned into an even greater challenge by making them into puzzle caches, where finding the cache (or, even, starting on the trail to it) depends on solving a puzzle: there is no limitation on the type of puzzle that can be used and people have set some very innovative and challenging problems.

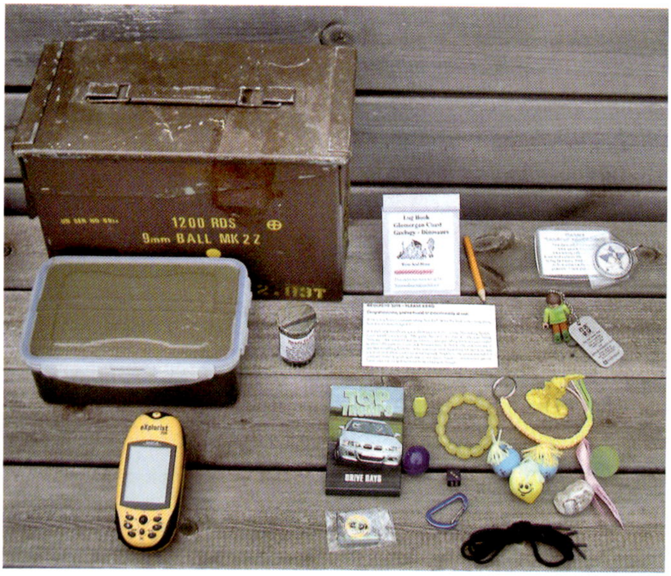

Paraphernalia of Geocaching – clockwise from top left: three examples of cache containers, Log Book and pencil, information sheet to explain what the cache is (in case of accidental find), Geocoin, Travel Bug and dog tag, typical collection of exchange items, and a GPS

Gordon Hindess

If this were not enough, people have introduced "travellers" who journey between caches, usually with a set mission. These are known as Travel Bugs and Geocoins and any finder can help them on their way by taking them to another cache. While there is no reasonable limit to what can be specified as a mission, one of the best examples is where a school class has released one and subsequently tracks its progress as part of a geography project. Sometimes groups of travellers are dispatched to race against each other, the goal being to get to a specified destination or travel the greatest distance in a set time. These races often start at Event Caches, which provide an opportunity for geocachers to get together for a day of fun.

Looking for a hidden box is not – and should not be – an end in itself. The objective is to attract people to places of interest, scenic value or with a linked story. The Victorian cemetery in Cathays fully meets this objective, containing memorials that provide glimpses of the City's history in a pleasant and peaceful park. Using the cemetery for a game is in keeping with the objectives of its Victorian founders who wanted it to be a pleasant an enjoyable place to visit, as well as a respectful final resting place for the citizens of Cardiff. Geocachers are expected to show appropriate respect for the cemetery during their visit but are also encouraged to enjoy, and explore further, the heritage and ecology.

A multicache was appropriate in this case, taking people on a tour of a little over half a mile and needing to find information at seven locations to determine the location of the final cache, in a small rectangular plastic container. This cache explores some of the more interesting memorials, where inscriptions give a greater insight into lives and circumstances, sometimes tragically, sometimes entertainingly. The graves visited not only feature prominent citizens, but also include the less well known who have contributed to the history of the city, local characters and some that simply tell an unusual tale.

If a further incentive to set up a cache here was needed, it was provided by a disabled geocacher from Dorset, who issued a challenge, through a "traveller", to set up wheelchair friendly caches. The Cathays Cemetery Cache was placed in 2007 specifically to meet this challenge in Cardiff.

In its first year, the cache was logged as found 34 times. As many cachers operate as pairs or families, this implies that more than fifty people were attracted to visit the cemetery. From their logs, all enjoyed the experience and most acknowledged that they would probably never have visited had it not been for the cache.

To find out more about geocaching, go to the website at www.geocaching.com which will take you to the global home page for the game. If you just want to find out about caches near you, put your postcode in the box provided and hit "Go". This will bring up a long list of caches in increasing order of distance from where you live. Clicking on any of these will bring up more details of the individual cache. If you are only interested in this cache, click on "HIDE and SEEK A CACHE" (top left on Home page), scroll down to "Other Search Options", put Cathays Cemetery in "by Keyword" and hit "Go". To obtain coordinates you will need to register as a member: there is no cost or commitment attached to this but, for reasons of personal security, you should do this using a pseudonym.

Gordon Hindess

CHAPTER FIVE

The Victorian Funeral

Surprisingly, little has changed in respect of the 'average' funeral. Whilst the majority of today's ritual takes place entirely at the crematorium, one hundred and fifty years ago the following scene could be witnessed in every town in Wales: the funeral car and mourning carriages would arrive at the house of the deceased, from which the coffin would be carried out and placed into the funeral car behind which the mourners would get into the carriages, in order of the closeness of their relationship with the deceased. Arriving at the cemetery, the coffin was shouldered into either the Anglican or the Nonconformist Chapel where the appropriate burial service would be read following which the coffin was taken to the grave for the committal. Depending on the distance between house and cemetery, the undertaker could have the entire panoply over within ninety minutes and be safely back at his premises.

Victorian Horse Drawn Hearse
Bereavement Services

Sub-contracting was common

Funerals were not always performed by the undertaker to whom one initially went. Messrs Banting, who held the royal warrant for funerals from 1805 to 1932, ceased making their own coffins in the 1860s when they decided that it was easier for them to contract out their manufacture than to keep joiners at their St James' premises for the sake of the fifteen or so funerals they were called upon to furnish each year. But it has to be understood that the investment required by a funeral furnisher to maintain his premises and equipage would have been substantial. For the lesser undertaker, most of his capital outlay could be recouped by hiring out his accoutrements to others within the trade. In 1843 Edwin Chadwick asked a Mr Dix, a successful London undertaker performing upwards of 800 funerals a year, to explain how the hiring-out system worked. Mr Dix said that he frequently performed funerals "three deep"; that is to say, he did it for one person who did it for another, though he himself might have been the person to whom the relatives of the deceased originally applied.

According to Chadwick, "The number of persons whose sole business (in London) is that of undertaker, whose names are enumerated in the post-office directory for the year 1843 for the metropolis, is 275. It is stated that much larger numbers than are named in the directory retain the insignia of undertakers in their shop windows, for the sake of the profits of one or two funerals a year. They merely transmit the orders of the furnishing undertakers, who supply materials and men at a comparatively low rate." The situation was no different in the provinces. Furthermore, it was not unusual for upholders to furnish funerals, in addition to their regular trade as interior decorators and auctioneers. The National Association of Funeral Directors Handbook for 1993 shows that, one hundred and fifty years on from Chadwick's observations, Greater London could still boast 163 funeral directors, being some 60% of the number so trading in 1843.

How was the Trade organised?

The trade had three branches: coffin-making, undertaking and funeral furnishing. The coffin-maker made coffins and might also have performed funerals. The undertaker bought his coffins from the coffin-maker, performing funerals for his artisan clients and tendering for pauper work. The funeral furnisher might have bought his coffins from a coffin-maker but it was more usual for him to have them made by his own staff who would then have furnished and upholstered them for his middle-class clients. This, then, was the hierarchy of the trade. The coffin-maker looked up to the undertaker and respected the funeral furnisher. The undertaker needed the coffin-maker and also respected the funeral furnisher. The funeral furnisher equally needed the coffin-maker, but he would have had little commerce with the undertaker.

CARDIFF CEMETERY, Cathays.

FEES AND CHARGES—In Consecrated Ground, including Cemetery Board charge, Grave digger, Incumbent, and Sexton, total for every interment—

				£	s.	d.
In Graves selected by the Board				1	1	4
Pauper				0	11	6
Child under 12 years of age				1	0	4
Still-born Child				0	2	6
Single Grave, space in perpetuity, 9 ft x 4 ft. not walled	£2	0	0			
For every interment	1	18	0			
				3	18	
Ditto 10 ft. x 4 ft	2	10	0			
For every interment	2	4	0			
				4	14	0
Double grave, space for vault, 9 ft. x 8 ft.	4	0	0			
For first interment	3	4	0			
				7	4	0
For every subsequent do.				2	4	0
Ditto 10 ft. x 8 ft.	5	0	0			
For first interment	3	6	0			
				8	6	0
For every subsequent ditto				2	4	0
For selection of site for unpurchased grave space				0	10	0
Ditto for vault or grave space in perpetuity				1	0	0
For permission to erect Headstone, not exceeding 4 feet in height, with or without curb stone on purchased grave space				0	10	0
Ditto to erect Flat stone on ditto				1	10	6
Ditto Ornamental tomb do.				3	1	0
Ditto Iron railing do.				3	3	0
For keeping Shrub or Flower beds in order, in perpetuity				2	0	0
For Turfing grave				0	3	0

For interment in Unconsecrated Ground the fees of Cemetery Board and grave digger's charge are the same as is in Consecrated ground; and the same fee is recommended for the Dissenting Minister as for the Incumbent.

An extra charge of half of Cemetery Board fee upon interment of non-parishioners.

Plan of the ground, showing situation of each grave, may be seen without charge at the office of the Cemetery Board, or at the Lodge of the Cemetery.

The Cemetery is open to the public daily. Certificates of Burial can only be obtained at the office of the Cemetery Board.

BENJAMIN MATTHEWS, Clerk.

Two handsome buildings, one eastward for Churchmen, the other westward for Dissenters, stand a short distance within the South entrance. Between the two rises a spire of considerable height, which is connected by archways with the buildings. A separate Chapel, north of the Cemetery, is appropriated to Roman Catholics. The archways over the entrance gates bear the arms of Cardiff and others; and a lodge for the keeper stands to the eastward, and the design of the whole has the impress of great good taste and ability.

Fees and Charges, Cathays Cemetery – Wakeford's Cardiff Directory, 1863

Cardiff Central Library

The Cost

That the Victorian funeral was expensive cannot be denied. From a total of £24,000,000 deposited with savings banks in 1843, between 25% and 30% of this – which is to say £6,000,000 to £8,000,000 – was saved in order to meet funeral expenses.

The 1843 *Government Commission on Burial in Towns*, edited by Edwin Chadwick, spoke with regret of "persons of inferior conditions and of limited means, who are governed by the examples of those above them, and who are put to ruinous expense." Furthermore, of the 43,000 funerals which had taken place in the metropolis in 1839, 23,000 were for those of children dying under the age of 10 years.

The Conduct of Funerals

The conduct of funerals was regulated by money and custom; the waste of the former and the overstepping of the latter provoked much censure. Funerals were sold on a sliding scale according to the social status of the deceased. This was unavoidable for the undertaker always visited his client to receive instructions. In this way, the undertaker was able to ascertain for certain the social status of the deceased from the address, the quality of furniture, fixtures and fittings within the house and the expense of his client's couture. The client, knowing that he was by now within the web of a sable spider, knew that there was little point in arguing the odds with the funeral furnisher. Indeed, as Dickens reminds us, funerals were frequently ordered by a resigned, "Provide that which is customary."

Victorian Hearse

Courtesy of Mark Evans, Llangadog, Victorian Carriage Master

The question arises as to whether or not the Victorian undertaker was aware of the significance of the many trappings he had at his command. During his visitation of funeral furnishing establishments in the early 1840s, Edwin Chadwick asked one of the London tradesmen:

> *"Are you aware that the array of funerals, commonly made by undertakers, is strictly the heraldic array of a baronial funeral. The two men who stand at the doors being supposed to be the two porters of the castle, with their staves, in black; the man who heads the procession, wearing a scarf, being representative of the herald-at-arms; the man who carries a plume of feathers on his head being an esquire, who bears the helm, with its plume of feathers; the pall-bearers with batons, being representatives of the knights-companion-at-arms; the men walking with wands being supposed to represent gentleman-ushers, with their wands; are you aware that this is the origin and type of the common array usually provided by those who undertake to perform funerals?"*
>
> To which the undertaker answered,
>
> *"No, I am not aware of it."*
>
> When asked if
>
> *"it may be presumed that those who order funerals are equally unaware of the incongruity for which such expense is incurred."*
>
> The undertaker agreed that they were almost certainly unaware.

Innate Conservatism

The mid-Victorian undertaker was probably the most un-innovative tradesman of the nineteenth century. There were so many openings they might have exploited, but it never occurred to them to do so. The manufacture of coffins, coffin-furniture and soft furnishings were independent trades relying solely on the funeral trade for their income. Only Dottridge Brothers of London and Ingall, Parsons & Clive of Birmingham offered a comprehensive funeral service to the private client, for they also traded as commercial undertakers as well as warehousemen. There was no assault made on the mourning stationery or mourning jewellery trades. And both Messrs Courtauld – whose fortune was based on their perfection of a fast dye for black crepe and a patented crepe-making machine – and Jay's Mourning Warehouse of Regent Street could rest assured that not one funeral furnisher concerned himself with buying into the business. Furthermore, no undertaker took advantage of private cemetery ownership; indeed, it was frequently the reverse, as Kensal Green, Highgate and Brookwood, in their earlier years, boasted their own undertaking establishments, chaplains and chapels thus offering a complete service to their clients.

A measure of social status

In an age when success was measured by material possessions and monetary wealth, the Victorian funeral was seen as an advertisement of the deceased's social status and rank. The trade was fully aware of this and established a sliding scale of charges through all

Victorian Hearse interior
Courtesy of Mark Evans, Llangadog, Victorian Carriage Master

levels of society, with the exception of those of the pauper class. An examination of the ledgers in Westminster Reference Library of J H Wick, an undertaker supplying contract funerals to the London Poor Law Union in the 1830s and 40s, shows that many relatives of the Union's deceased inmates took advantage of the caveat of rescuing the deceased from the ignominy of a pauper funeral by contributing an additional six shillings for the provision of a nameplate, the attendance of a mute and use of the best pall. Those who could not had to be content with a plain pine guinea coffin and four bearers at 3s 6d each.

Coffins

To meet the needs of the various social classes, there were two distinct types of coffin available throughout the Victorian period. Those for earth burial were of the single wooden shell variety, whereas those destined for deposit in a brick grave, vault, catacomb or mausoleum were triple shell, being an inner wooden coffin of elm, sealed within a coffin of 4lb lead – which is to say, sheet lead weighing 4lb per square foot – itself placed within an outer wooden case constructed of 1½ in planks. The reason for such elaborate production on the part of the triple shell coffin was to guard against the leaching of any fluids or gasses associated with decomposition; it had nothing whatsoever to do with the preservation of the remains. Indeed, arterial sanitisation, or 'embalming' as it is erroneously called, was a late introduction to England from America in the 1890s and even then it was only used on cases destined for repatriation. These triple coffins were bulky affairs, weighing between 4 and 5 hundredweight, requiring a minimum of eight men to handle them.

The advent of an elaborate ritual

With the advent of the joint stock cemetery companies in the 1830s the need for vehicle transport was a vital necessity. Now, with reasonably long distances to cover, and travelling through a number of districts, the trade perfected elaborate spectacle for the public to see. In actuality, they were more an advertisement for their own establishment than for the comfort of the mourners. Mutes, feathers, attendants, mourning carriages and horse-velvets did not come cheap.

A slow and sombre pace was maintained as the procession moved away from the house, but once it had rounded the corner the horse-velvets were unhooked and the cavalcade proceeded to the cemetery at a reasonably brisk trot. As the cemetery gates came into view the horse-velvets were reattached and the procession slowed down. Entering the gates the mutes would take their station at the head of the cortege, the bearers with their brass-capped tipstaffs would flank the funeral car, three a side. All was then ready for the off and, with the leading horses reigned to prance their way to the chapel, the procession began the last part of its dismal journey. With the service over, the coffin was returned to the funeral car for the short transfer to the graveside. As the burial itself was taking place, the funeral car – the horses now without their velvets – was on its ways back to the carriage-master's premises, leaving only the carriages to take the mourners back from where the procession had begun.

Later developments

It would be wrong to assume that the Victorians relished elaborate funerary ritual. They, like us, were victims of trade advertising and a desire to keep up appearances. It was the funeral trade who set the standard, ingeniously selling funerals on a sliding scale according to the social status of the deceased. It was they who ensured that death was made as much a public spectacle as money could buy. Today's simpler funerals would have been envied by the Victorians, but it was not until the 1880s that we see a demanding clientele, seeking quality and dignity rather than tawdry excesses. Thus it was that the middle classes brought about the change, patronising only those firms who understood their desire for a simplified ritual. It was left to those lower down the social scale to adopt the type of ostentatious display abandoned by those higher up the scale. Some funeral furnishers were only too willing to service this demand – after all, they had a need to recoup their outlay. So came into being the vulgar pomp of the East London funerals of the late nineteenth century that remain – erroneously – in the public's mind as the epitome of the Victorian funeral. But it was at a cost, for those undertakers willing to down-status their patrons lost the trade of the middle classes.

Julian W S Litten

CHAPTER SIX

Nature and Biodiversity

Cemeteries are sometimes referred to as the 'green lungs' of a city as they are often the only area within a city boundary where the natural habitat is allowed to thrive. Ecology is encouraged in the cemetery by a variety of means, including selective planting, adopting differing grass cutting regimes and limiting the use of weedkiller. In 2002, a conservation policy was established, aiming to create and preserve a natural habitat for wildlife and enable natural plants and flowers to flourish. The policy leaves five large sections within the oldest part of the cemetery as conservation areas, where the grass is not cut during the summer months but allowed to grow encouraging the native flora and fauna to flourish. A long grass habitat ensures an abundant supply of seed heads which provide a much needed food source. By not cutting the grass some of the less common creatures, such as the slow worm which might be killed by strimming equipment, are able to thrive.

Slowworm
Gordon Hindess

Do not be fooled by the rotting log pile: this is not just a case of failure to tidy up after tree clearance. Healthy and rotting wood provide habitats for a wide variety of 'mini-beasts', as well as for fungi. If you do not believe this, feel free to turn logs over to look, but remember to return them carefully to their original position. Encouragement of a healthy environment for insects in turn attracts birds, including magpies, robins, blue tits, tree creepers, wrens, green woodpeckers and, occasionally, the sparrow hawk.

Green woodpecker
Via Tony Price

Memorials made from stone are not just of interest to geologists. Environmental scientists may study the weathering of a memorial from the date it was erected to the present day, revealing the effect of pollution. Colourful lichens may also populate memorials.

So, while you enjoy the diverse range of trees and the displays of wild flowers, listen to the birdsong and look out for bees, beetles, butterflies and moths, birds and mammals such as squirrels, hedgehogs or, perhaps, the urban fox. In the remainder of this chapter we will look at some specific aspects of the natural history which can be found in the cemetery.

Trees

When the cemetery was laid out, the initial plantings were of evergreen trees. In later Victorian times more native deciduous trees were added, to reflect changing attitudes. Each tree was labelled with both the English and Latin names for the tree. Successive generations have continued to reflect the views of their age, producing a variety of trees that amount to an arboretum. The trees also cater for all the seasons.

In the winter, there are sufficient evergreens to ensure continuity of greenery. These trees include the Monkey Puzzle, or Chile Pine, Common and Irish Yew, Cypress, Black and Scots Pine, Holm (or Evergreen) Oak, Holly (with Ivy adding to the festive atmosphere!) and Cedar of Lebanon. The last of these stands in splendour in its own roundabout at the back of the chapels.

Monkey Puzzle
Bereavement Services

Spring Blossoms

Gordon Hindess

Magnolia

Ornamental pear

Crab apple

Cherry

In the spring, colourful blossoms are provided by Ornamental Pear, Cherry, Crab Apple, Magnolia, Rowan, the Wayfaring Tree and Sweet Briar. The last of these has pretty bright pink flowers, with a fragrance closely resembling apples, a smell more evident during warm and showery weather.

Traditional deciduous trees come into their own during the summer. These include Oak, Beech, Sycamore, Field Maple, Ash, Birch, Whitebeam and Lime. Limes have yellow-green delicately scented blossom which is much favoured by bees, while a soothing tea can be brewed from both fresh and dried flowers, to be taken with lemon and sugar.

In the autumn, the bright berries on the Wayfaring Tree and Whitebeam provide early colour, which is followed by the full autumn hues as the leaves change colour, notably on the Field Maple, Beech and, again, the Wayfaring Tree. While on the subject of leaf colour, we should not forget the magnificent Copper Beech and the Golden Scots Pine, which glows in sunlight. Also during the autumn a rich harvest of fruit arrives to feed the birds and animals through the coming winter, including acorns, hazel nuts, beech mast and pine cones.

As an example of how trees can be cropped, there are two coppiced Willow stools. The wood would have been used for diverse purposes, ranging from gateposts to wattle, in fencing and wall (wattle and daub) construction. Coppicing is an on-going process, involving the cutting down of branches so that new shoots grow up from the cut stumps. Wood can be taken from the same tree over and over again for many years.

Bats

Cathays Cemetery provides many opportunities for bats to forage and rest. The species likely to be found are Pipistrelle (Common and Soprano), Noctule and Brown Long-eared bats. All of these feed on flying insects found mainly around the tops of trees and over long grass areas. You are most likely to see a Noctule bat, a large species with a wingspan of up to 40cm, flying around just before sunset. Sometimes Pipistrelles come out just as it is getting dark and you will be able to see the difference in size as they only have a wingspan of 25cm.

To encounter most species it is probably easiest to join one of the regular bat walks, where there will be experts with bat detectors. These convert the high-pitched noises made by bats into audible noises that we can hear. Each species has a different call: Noctules have a low 'chip chop' call, Pipistrelles a busy series of clicks and Brown Long-eared bats have a quiet click like a Geiger counter.

Contrary to popular belief most species of bat in the UK do not sleep hanging upside-down, but prefer to tuck themselves into small gaps such as under roof tiles or behind tree bark. There are many trees in the cemetery that are suitable for bats to use as roost sites. They may also use surrounding houses and come to feed in the cemetery.

Geology

Rock outcrops within the urban environment are generally in short supply so geologists may have to look to the man-made environment to satisfy their interests. Within urban areas cemeteries with their stone headstones and memorials are of particular interest as, depending upon their age, they can offer an insight into the local geology as well as providing the opportunity to examine a variety of different rock types from all over the world. Cathays Cemetery has just such a rich geological heritage, offering examples of local as well as far more exotic rock types that reflect improvement in transport and changes in fashion.

There are three major groups of rocks: igneous, metamorphic and sedimentary, and examples of all three occur in the cemetery. Igneous rocks begin their existence as molten magma deep in the Earth's crust that on cooling generally forms hard, crystalline rocks that take a good polish. There are many different varieties, some coarsely crystalline, others with crystals so small that they are impossible to detect individually with the naked eye. The size of the crystals reflects how long the rock has taken to cool; the larger the crystals the longer it has taken to cool, which in turn is a measure of the depth of origin in the Earth's crust. As well as varying in crystal size, igneous rocks also differ in their mineral composition due to variations in the chemical make up of the magma from which they were produced.

Pink granite, Billups memorial
Stephen Howe

Close up of pink granite with "heathen". The heathen is a foreign stone which was picked up by the magma before it came to rest and solidified
Stephen Howe

No igneous rocks crop out around Cardiff, so those found within the cemetery have been brought in from farther afield. Granites, with their large crystals are commonly used and many varieties of these have been used for headstones within the cemetery. Commonly seen are light coloured granites, which can be seen in the memorials to Jim Driscoll, Ernest Willows and William Seager. Many originate from Cornwall, but during the C19th and early part of the C20th, red and pink granites from the Aberdeen district were very much in vogue. As these quarries declined, similar rocks began to be imported from Scandinavia. Examples of such pink and red granites can be seen in the memorials to Jonathan Billups, Andrew Pettigrew and William Reardon Smith.

Today, due to cheap costs, we can find headstones made from rocks originating from many parts of the world. Many of these can be seen in the modern memorial area where black 'granites' (these are not granites but finer-grained dark igneous rocks) rub shoulders with a variety of other 'exotic' stones. Of these, Larvikite from southern Norway is particularly distinctive, and is characterized by large blue crystals that when polished, shimmer in the light. Examples can be seen amongst the modern memorials, and it has also been used for the plaque on the memorial to the French sailors.

Sedimentary rocks can be divided into two main groups: those composed from particles derived from the weathering of pre-existing rocks (e.g. sandstones) and those formed from the accumulation of fossil shells, the lime taken from seawater by organisms such as corals and bivalves (e.g. limestones). Sedimentary rocks are generally much softer than igneous rocks, but often far easier to work, especially before the development of modern machinery. Cardiff and southeast Wales is underlain by different types of sedimentary rocks and a number of these can be found within the cemetery. Pennant Sandstone, which crops out over much of the South Wales coalfield has been used extensively as a building stone, as in the main walls of the cemetery chapel and entrance gate. It commonly occurs as thin, flaggy beds and this property and its rough, hard-wearing surface has led to its use for paving stones. It was also widely used for headstones in the C18th and C19th. In order to get a large, flat surface for this purpose, the thin slabs have to be turned on end, which can cause them to weather badly, as this allows rainwater to penetrate between the individual rock layers; when this freezes in winter it expands and splits them apart. A good example of this can be seen on the rear surface of the memorial to John Wall.

Pennant Sandstone, showing flaking due to weathering
Gordon Hindess

Pink granite cross on Radyr Stone pedestal, George Henry Elliott grave
Gordon Hindess

Close up of Radyr Stone
Gordon Hindess

There are a few examples in the cemetery of Radyr Stone, a rock that is unique to Cardiff. This very coarse sedimentary rock is full of generally angular pebbles of hard grey Carboniferous Limestone set in a red-coloured, sandy matrix. It crops out on the banks of the River Taff at Radyr, and has been widely used as decorative stone in Cardiff, especially for capping stones on walls and for kerb stones. A nice headstone made of this rock, inscribed to Lizzie Kennedy, can be seen between those to Jonathan Billups and Andrew Pettigrew.

A number of limestones occur in the vicinity of Cardiff, but the most extensive are the hard, grey Carboniferous Limestones that crop out around the edge of the coalfield and, in the Vale of Glamorgan, the blue-grey limestones of the Jurassic Blue Lias that are well exposed along the coast. Both have been used widely in local buildings, but less often for memorial work due to their hardness and difficulty in working. An example of Carboniferous Limestone can be seen in the cross on top of the Irish Famine memorial although this is not local, having been imported from Ireland.

Portland Stone, which originates from Dorset, is a renowned building stone. This pale, creamy-white limestone is easily worked, hard wearing and can be dressed into a smooth surface to take inscriptions. It was chosen by Wren to rebuild London after the Great Fire of 1666, and has been used for numerous public buildings, including those in Cardiff's Civic Centre. It was also the stone selected by the Commonwealth War Graves Commission for its headstones. Careful examination of these will often reveal the fossil remains of oysters. Examples can be seen in the World War II grave area and the headstone of Major Valliant de Guelis.

Metamorphic rocks are those that since their original state have been changed by heat and/or pressure. The amount of alteration varies enormously, and at the extreme produces rocks that have almost been re-melted due to the intense heat and pressure to which they have been subjected, deep in the Earth's crust. Two types of metamorphic rock that can be seen in the cemetery are slate and marble.

Slate is a mud rock that has been compressed to the point where it is in the order of 60% thinner than it was originally. During this process, the distinctive 'slaty cleavage' – the way the rock splits into thin sheets – is formed. Slates are easily cut into slabs, hard wearing and smooth faced, and so are ideal for headstones. Many would originally have come from north Wales, but these days they can be imported from many parts of the world. An example of slate to be seen on the Heritage Trail is the plaque on the face of the Irish Famine Memorial.

True marble is a metamorphosed limestone, although quarrymen use the term to describe any limestone that can take a good polish. Marble has a sugary texture and its soft nature allows delicate carving. It takes a good polish, can be relatively hard wearing and can occur in a variety of colours. White marble is one of the commonest forms, and many of the white marbles come from the Carrara region of northern Italy. Marble has been used for centuries as a building and statuary stone and is commonly to be seen as memorial sculptures inside churches. The headstone of Louisa Maud Evans is an example of a white marble memorial.

Carboniferous Limestone cross (Irish Famine memorial). Plaque in pedestal is slate

Stephen Howe

Cathays Cemetery has a rich geological heritage in its memorials and headstones, and the rock types described above are only a small fraction of those that can be seen. Generally, the rocks used for the older memorials are of local, or at least of British origin, and reflect the fashion of the day, or accessibility of the source. Tastes change; today, Carrara Marble 'angels' and 'anchors of hope' are less fashionable whilst deeply coloured granites and metamorphic rocks are currently popular and with cheap bulk transport, you can find rock types originating from all over the world.

Gordon Hindess
Laura Palmer (Bats)
Stephen Howe (Geology)

CHAPTER SEVEN

Welsh Inscriptions in Cathays Cemetery

There are many Welsh inscriptions in Cathays, particularly in the sections to the left of the main entrance, in that part of the cemetery which was used by nonconformists. Some of them are completely in Welsh, but we also find, as is common throughout Wales, a tendency to give the factual details in English and then to add a Biblical verse or poem in Welsh. It may seem odd that people would mix the two languages like this, but we have to remember that for many years English was the only language with official status. There may well have been a feeling that the formal record of the death should therefore be in English, though with the option of adding a poem or verse in Welsh as well.

Some of those commemorated with a Welsh gravestone were clearly leaders of the community, ministers and deacons of the Welsh chapels in Cardiff, but information about the working lives of those commemorated is scarce. We find a few seamen and teachers, but the general impression is of ordinary working people who didn't feel that the jobs they had been doing were of any particular interest. On the whole they lived in Cathays or the Docks, according to the addresses given in the inscriptions, particularly in the early days. What is perhaps more interesting is how many of them were originally from West Wales – from Pembrokeshire or Cardiganshire. There are references to St David's, St Dogmael's, Aberystwyth, New Quay and many other places along the coast. We can see how Welsh-speakers from the west were moving to Cardiff, but retaining their identity.

Even so, there are occasionally inscriptions commemorating people with some public standing in the wider world. Perhaps the most interesting of these is Sir John Rowland who died in 1941, aged 63. The inscription tells us that he was a loving father, originally from Tregaron, and notes his various decorations – CB, CBE, MVO, YH (= JP). What it does not say, and we have to search for this information elsewhere, is that he was a civil servant who worked closely with David Lloyd George, and was part of the early developments which led up to what we now call 'the welfare state'.

The Welsh inscriptions in Cathays often include a poem which has clearly been written specially to commemorate the individual buried there, not necessarily great literature, but revealing the love and respect felt by family and friends. Others include a verse or even a single line from the work of a well-known poet, but are surprisingly ready to adapt the wording. There seems to have been a feeling, here as elsewhere in Wales, that such poems were a resource to be used as the needs of the family might require.

One popular example is a line from a poem by Evan Evans, better known by his bardic name Ieuan Glan Geirionnydd. It may appear in the correct, original form as: "A'u hun mor dawel yw" *And their sleep is so peaceful,* very appropriate where the inscription refers to several people. Where only one person is commemorated, however, the line is readily changed to "A'i hun mor dawel yw" *And his/her sleep is so peaceful.* Even Biblical verses may

Brynmor Johns' gravestone: This inscription includes an 'englyn', a traditional form of Welsh poetry often used on gravestones. It consists of four lines which must be in turn of ten, six, seven and seven syllables. The seventh syllable of the first line introduces the rhyme, which then appears in the last syllable of the other lines

Yn yr arysgrif hon fe welir englyn, un o ffurfiau traddodiadol barddoniaeth Gymraeg a ddefnyddir yn aml ar gerrig beddi. Mae'r llinellau yn eu tro yn ddeg, chwech, saith a saith sillaf. Daw'r odl ar ddiwedd seithfed sillaf y llinell gyntaf, ac wedyn yn sillaf olaf y llinellau eraill

Eric R Fletcher

be subject to this process. One which is normally used to commemorate a woman is "Hyn a allodd hon hi a'i gwnaeth" *She hath done what she could* [Mark 14.8], but if the deceased was a man we find instead "Hyn a allodd hwn, efe a'i gwnaeth" *He hath done what he could.* There is no Biblical basis for this form, but this kind of adaptation was clearly felt to be appropriate and acceptable

These inscriptions are an interesting record of the Welsh-speaking community in Cardiff in the later years of the Nineteenth Century and the first half of the Twentieth. Ordinary people who came to Cardiff as it developed into a town and then a city, but nevertheless retained their language and culture.

Arysgrifau Cymraeg ym Mynwent Cathays

Mae nifer fawr o arysgrifau Cymraeg yn y fynwent hon, yn enwedig yn y rhan lle cleddid yr anghydffurfwyr, i'r chwith o'r brif fynedfa. Cymraeg yw pob gair yn rhai arysgrifau, ond mae yma duedd, fel ym mhob rhan o Gymru, i gyflwyno'r manylion ffeithiol yn Saesneg ac wedyn ychwanegu adnod neu bennill yn Gymraeg. Wrth geisio deall y rheswm am hyn, rhaid i ni gofio mai'r Saesneg am flynyddoedd lawer oedd yr unig iaith â statws swyddogol. Tybed a ddatblygodd rhyw deimlad bod angen i'r cofnod ffurfiol fod yn Saesneg, er bod ychwanegu pennill neu adnod yn Gymraeg wedyn yn berffaith dderbyniol?

Roedd rhai o'r bobl a goffeir â charreg fedd Gymraeg yn flaenllaw yn y gymdeithas, gweinidogion a deaconiaid y capeli Cymraeg yng Nghaerdydd, ond ychydig iawn a wyddom am waith pob dydd y rhan fwyaf o'r bobl a goffeir. Fe welwn fod ambell un yn forwr, yn athro neu yn athrawes, ond yr argraff a gawn yw mai pobl gyffredin oedd y rhain, yn teimlo nad oedd eu gwaith o unrhyw ddiddordeb arbennig. Ar y cyfan roeddent yn byw yn Cathays neu yn y Dociau, yn ôl y cyfeiriadau a roddir yn yr arysgrifau, yn arbennig yn y dyddiau

An example of a bilingual memorial
Enghraifft o gofeb ddwyieithog
Eric R Fletcher

cynnar. Mwy trawiadol efallai yw bod cymaint ohonynt yn dod yn wreiddiol o'r gorllewin – o Sir Benfro neu Sir Aberteifi. Mae yna gyfeiriadau at Dyddewi, Llandudoch, Aberystwyth, Cei Newydd a nifer o fannau eraill ar hyd yr arfordir. Gallwn weld y Cymry Cymraeg o'r gorllewin yn symud i Gaerdydd, ond yn cadw eu hymlyniad at eu milltir sgwâr.

Fodd bynnag, mae yma ambell arysgrif yn coffáu pobl oedd â statws yn y gymdeithas ehangach. Y mwyaf diddorol o'r rhain efallai yw Sir John Rowland a fu farw yn 1941, yn 63 oed. Mae'r arysgrif yn nodi ei fod yn dad a phriod annwyl, a'i fod yn dod yn wreiddiol o Dregaron, ac mae'n rhestru'r anrhydeddau a roddwyd iddo – CB, CBE, MVO, YH. Nid yw'n datgelu, a rhaid i ni chwilota am y wybodaeth hon mewn ffynonellau eraill, ei fod yn was sifil a gydweithiodd yn agos â David Lloyd George, ac a oedd yn rhan o'r datblygiadau cynnar arweiniodd yn y pen draw at yr hyn a elwir heddiw yn 'wladwriaeth les'.

Mae nifer o'r arysgrifau Cymraeg yn cynnwys pennill a luniwyd, mae'n amlwg, yn unswydd i goffáu'r person a gladdwyd yno. Nid yw'r rhain fel arfer o werth llenyddol arbennig, ond maent yn dangos yn glir y cariad a'r parch a deimlid gan deulu a chydnabod. Dro arall mae yna bennill neu linell o waith bardd adnabyddus, a thipyn o syndod yw gweld pa mor barod oedd pobl i newid geiriad y rhain. Mae'n amlwg eu bod yn teimlo, yma yng Nghaerdydd fel mewn ardaloedd eraill, bod perffaith hawl ganddynt i ddefnyddio ac addasu'r cerddi hyn yn ôl anghenion y teulu.

Un enghraifft boblogaidd yw llinell o gerdd gan Evan Evans, neu Ieuan Glan Geirionnydd a defnyddio'i enw barddol. Y ffurf wreiddiol, gywir yw "A'u hun mor dawel yw". Mae'n briodol iawn pan fydd yr arysgrif yn cyfeirio at nifer o bobl, ac fe'i gwelir yn aml yn y fynwent. Lle coffeir un person yn unig, fe newidir y llinell yn rhwydd i "A'i hun mor dawel yw". Gall hyd yn oed adnodau o'r Beibl dderbyn yr un driniaeth. Adnod a ddefnyddir fel arfer i goffáu gwraig yw "Hyn a allodd hon hi a'i gwnaeth" [Marc 14.8], ond lle mae'r arysgrif yn coffáu dyn, fe welwn yn hytrach "Hyn a allodd hwn, efe a'i gwnaeth". Nid oes unrhyw sail Feiblaidd i'r ffurf hon, ond mae'n amlwg y teimlai pobl fod addasu adnodau fel hyn yn briodol ac yn dderbyniol.

Mae'r arysgrifau yn y fynwent yn gofnod diddorol o'r gymuned Gymraeg yng Nghaerdydd yn ail hanner y bedwaredd ganrif ar bymtheg a hanner cyntaf yr ugeinfed ganrif. Pobl gyffredin ddaeth i Gaerdydd mewn cyfnod pan oedd yn datblygu'n dref ac wedyn yn ddinas, ond a gadwodd eu haith a'u diwylliant.

Gwen Awbery

CHAPTER EIGHT

War Graves

To most of us perhaps the most evocative image of military headstones is a view of one of the many World War I cemeteries in Flanders: row on row of uniform white memorials, where the relatively modest size and simplicity accentuate the effect. Grander memorials often dwarf such headstones when they are scattered around cemeteries in this country and this is often the case at Cathays. However, there are over 500 war graves in Cathays Cemetery, with most marked by a distinctive small headstone.

War Graves with memorial cross, all maintained by the War Graves Commission

Bereavement Services

The reason for the uniformity of the memorials is that they were provided by the Commonwealth War Graves Commission, which was established by Royal Charter in 1917. The Commission was charged with the duty to mark and maintain the graves of members of the Commonwealth forces killed in the First World War, to build memorials to those with no known burial place and to keep records and registers. Sadly, it has been necessary to extend the duty through a second world war and to numerous other conflicts around the globe. The Commission's principles are that the dead should be commemorated individually by name and that each memorial is permanent and uniform, with no distinction made on account of rank, race or creed. Each headstone is 2′ 8″ in height and is made of Portland stone. A national emblem, regimental or service badge is engraved at the top of the memorial, followed by rank, name, unit, date of death and age, with an appropriate religious emblem at the foot.

The memorials in Cathays Cemetery represent all branches of the services. While the Welch Regiment and Welsh Guards are well represented, reflecting the proximity of Maindy Barracks, examination of the insignia on the memorials shows that local people served in regiments across the country.

Insignia of both the Royal and Merchant Navies can be found: the latter is not surprising when you remember that various Cardiff based commercial vessels were involved in World War II. Paddle steamers of the P and A Campbell Line rescued over 7,000 troops during the Dunkirk evacuations of 1940, while the William Reardon Smith Line lost over 20 vessels through enemy action.

War Graves Commission headstone, with insignia of the Welch Regiment
Gordon Hindess

One of the more unusual insignias is that the General List, which was often used in war time to speed up the process of commissioning officers. The list also includes those who did not wish to highlight their allegiances because, for example, they were involved with the Special Operations Executive. One of these was Major Jacques Vaillant de Guelis whose Cardiff family were involved in the export of Welsh coal to Brittany. Jacques was bi-lingual and became the personal interpreter for the Commanding Officer of the British Expeditionary Force. Following the liberation of France, he was assigned to the Special Allied Airborne Recce Force to help co-ordinate local resistance and provide intelligence feedback, especially concerning conditions in prisoner of war and concentration camps. During this work he was injured in a car accident and died.

It is important to remember that both men and women lost their lives in the wars: the graves of some WAAFs can be found in Cathays Cemetery. The Woman's Auxiliary Air Force came into existence in June 1939 and made a tremendous contribution to the victory gained in 1945. Women took over the roles of airmen, releasing them for active duties. A wide range of roles included driving RAF transport and working in Operations Rooms and as radio operators.

Mention must also be made of the foreign nationals for whom this cemetery is their final resting place. These include 21 French sailors who died whilst serving in the French navy during the Great War. The individual graves, the majority of which are in the Roman

Stone cross with bronze plaque on grave of French sailor
Gordon Hindess

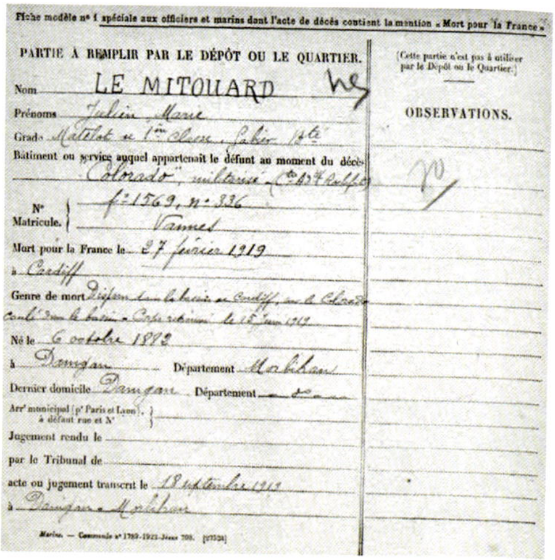

Fiche modèle nº 1 spéciale aux officiers et marins dont l'acte de décès contient la mention « Mort pour la France »

PARTIE À REMPLIR PAR LE DÉPÔT OU LE QUARTIER.

(Cette partie n'est pas à utiliser par le Dépôt ou le Quartier.)

OBSERVATIONS.

Nom LE MITOUARD

Prénoms Julien Marie

Grade Matelot de 1re classe

Bâtiment ou service auquel appartenait le défunt au moment du décès "Colorado"

Nº Matricule. fº 1569, nº 336 Vannes

Mort pour la France le 27 février 1919

à Cardiff

Genre de mort [illegible]

Né le 6 octobre 1892

à Damgan Département Morbihan

Dernier domicile Damgan Département do

Arrᵗ municipal (pʳ Paris et Lyon), à défaut rue et Nº

Jugement rendu le

par le Tribunal de

acte ou jugement transcrit le 18 septembre 1919

à Damgan Morbihan

Death Certificate of French sailor 'Died for France on 27 February 1919 at Cardiff'
French Military Archive

Catholic section, are marked by stone crosses with bronze plaques bearing the details. It had been a wish of the French community in Cardiff to honour the sailors with a memorial and, in November 1998, the Vice Consul General unveiled a granite tablet bearing the Tricolour and an inscription in gold leaf. The memorial was kindly donated by the memorial masons, Mossfords.

Families do not have to accept the standard headstone provided by the War Graves Commission, so some graves of military personal are of more conventional and unique style. An example of this is the memorial to John Cleal, a 23 year old stoker who postponed his wedding to take part in the Zeebrugge raid in 1918, but was fatally wounded. The memorial was provided by public subscription, in recognition of his sacrifice while putting duty and loyalty to his shipmates before his personal interests. His grave was recently re-discovered by the Friends and a simple, but moving re-dedication took place in February 2008.

Re-dedication of John Cleal memorial, February 2008
Nicholas Davey

Graves dating from before the First World War pre-date the introduction of the uniform Portland Stone headstone. One such memorial is that to William Llewellyn Rhys, a vicar's son from Llantrisant, who achieved the rank of Troop Sergeant Major but was also demoted twice. He went to America to fight in the Civil War and, if we can interpret the quote from Alfred Lord Tennyson's poem which appears on the memorial, it would appear that he was one of the few survivors of the Charge of the Light Brigade in the Crimean War.

This chapter gives a brief glimpse of the military graves in Cathays Cemetery. The Insignia Trail Guide, produced by Cardiff Council's Bereavement Services, takes you to twenty of the memorials bearing the insignia of various forces who fought during the World Wars. The Guide contains information describing the Regimental emblems and the activities of the forces during the wars.

Gordon Hindess

CHAPTER NINE

Beginnings

The First Interment

There is no surviving tombstone in memory of the first interment at Cathays Cemetery. Originally I feel sure there would have been, the eldest daughter of such a high ranking family, her father was Spanish Consul, would warrant some form of monument, especially being buried so far from her native-country. Perhaps it was just another victim of World War II bombing, or maybe just time has erased any reminder of its position. The date was July 10th, 1859. The service had been in Latin, the preferred language of the Roman Catholic Church.

Juan de Pico stood at the graveside, his two sons beside him, fighting back tears he said his final goodbyes:

"Adios mi querida hija, nuestra adorada Marcia"

There was little sound, only the stamping of the black plumed horses, the noise of the harnesses as they shook their heads, keeping away flies on a hot summer's day. On the breeze could be heard the distant barking of sheepdogs on Crwys Farm.

"Hasta que nos encontremos neuvamente en el cielo"

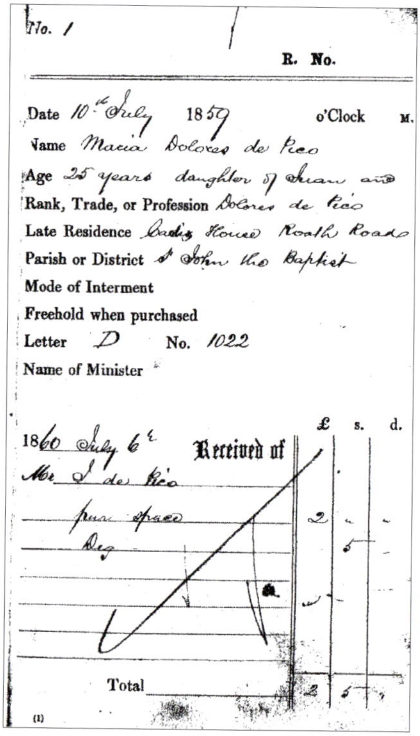
No. 1

R. No.

Date 10th July 1859 o'Clock M.

Name Maria Dolores de Pico

Age 25 years daughter of Juan and

Rank, Trade, or Profession Dolores de Pico

Late Residence Cadiz House Roath Roads

Parish or District St John the Baptist

Mode of Interment

Freehold when purchased

Letter D No. 1022

Name of Minister

1860 July 6th Received of Mr J de Pico

Total

Receipt for the burial of Maria Dolores de Pico. The address of the deceased is given as Cadiz House, Roath Road. This site was later occupied by the Oddfellows Institute in the re-named Newport Road

Bereavement Services

After shaking hands with the other mourners, a few friends from his native Spain but mainly members from Cardiff's other two dozen or so Consulates, he returned home to his grief-stricken wife and silent respectful servants.

Moving forward to the present day, Cardiff is once again the home of an increasing number of Consul officials. Thirty countries, mainly European, have officers in Wales. Two are full-time career Consular officials, the other twenty-eight being honorary officers. Together they form the Welsh Diplomatic Corps, surely recognition of the increasing international standing of both Cardiff as a City and of Wales as a Country.

Left: Memorial of Cornelious Hatch (and his wife)
Below: Inscription on Cornelious Hatch Memorial
Nicholas Davey

Cornelious Hatch

This is the memorial stone to one of the first Managers of Cathays Cemetery, Mr. Cornelious Hatch who died, aged 69, in December 1880. He lived in Fairoak Lodge adjacent to the main cemetery entrance. The stone was recently uncovered by Friends of Cathays Cemetery during laurel and bramble clearing.

Eric R Fletcher

CHAPTER TEN

Aerial Exploits

Balloon Girl

Her body was pulled from the mud at about midnight and laid in the bell tower of the local church. Monday morning it was solemnly borne across the road to the Waterloo Inn where the district coroner presided over the inquest. The jury, after much deliberation, returned to the packed main bar where on the direction of the coroner the foreman rose to his feet.

"Our unanimous verdict is, that the deceased was accidentally drowned in the Bristol Channel whilst attempting to descend by parachute from a balloon"

He paused and turned to face the coroner and continued,

"We also wish to censor Mr Gaudron, showman and balloon aeronaut, in that he showed great carelessness and disregard for the safety of such a young girl by allowing her to attempt her descent during such high winds"

How did such a young lady, aged 14, come to jump from the harness of a balloon 5,000 feet above the coastal reaches of what is now known as Cardiff Bay?

The year was 1896, the month July and a large Exhibition was being held in the area of what is now Cathays Park. There were stalls, exhibitors, some serious, others just there to relive poor hard-working people of their money and, as nowadays, all manner of food and drinks stalls. The daily highlight of the Cardiff Industrial and Maritime Exhibition [as it was grandly called] was the evening ascent by balloon followed by a parachute descent, the brave aeronaut landing without harm on the City's outskirts. He would then be collected by horse drawn carriage to make a triumphant return to the Exhibition field.

Why did this young girl become involved in such a potentially dangerous occupation?

Mr Gaudron had advertised for a young lady assistant for 'balloon' work and Mlle Albertina, as this girl choose to call herself was a successful applicant. When questioned by a local paper Mr Gaudron was asked,

"How long have you been acquainted with her?"

He replied,

"About four months, I do not know much about her. She says she has a mother but I don't know of any other relatives. She is working quite alone and for herself".

He continued,

"She first went up in a captive balloon with me at Dublin, then started parachuting in Cornwall, at Redruth. Last night's descent was her sixth. She has never fallen in the sea before but she is a good swimmer".

The previous evening M Gaudron had made a successful jump, landing near Roath Park, less than half a mile from Cathays Cemetery and what was to become Mlle Albertina's final resting place. Many hundreds of people, mainly on foot, some on horseback, street urchins, mothers running with prams, they all followed the path of the balloon hoping to catch a glimpse of the brave aeronaut slowly descending to a safe landing. Quoting from a local paper, "thousands of men, women and children made their appearance as if by magic, panting and blowing and flushed with heat and eagerness to get a close view of the descent".

The arrangement was that M Gaudron and Mlle Albertina would jump on alternate evenings. The next evening the crowds were even bigger. The roads of Adamsdown, Roath and Splott, even as far as Cardiff Docks were packed with jostling crowds. The cliffs at Penarth were lined with families, many having brought sandwiches, lemonade for the children, beer for the men. A stiff wind had blown away the threatening clouds leaving a clear blue sky. A lovely evening for a picnic. A male aeronaut was one thing, but a 14-year-old girl, that was something else. Something not to be missed.

A local paper described her as young and diminutive, a pretty little woman with girlish blue eyes. She was wearing a sailor suit, an ominous choice as it turned out. It all began as planned. To rapturous cheers and loud shouts wishing her good luck, she took her seat beneath the balloon and, caught by a stiff breeze, was well above the houses in a matter of seconds. From eye witness reports it would seem that when she was above the Roath area and travelling at great speed over Newport Road, over the Infirmary towards the Docks and open sea beyond, the wind suddenly dropped which caused the balloon to rapidly gain height. One spectator likened it to an aerial exclamation mark. Mlle Albertina being the rapidly diminishing dot below. It was not until well over 5,000 feet that she released herself from the balloon harness. As to what happened next we can only rely on newspaper reports, of which there were many, from an engine driver at the Bute dock bringing down coal wagons, numerous boatmen, ships officers, fishermen and an assortment of Cardiff and Penarth residents. Their accounts vary as to the exact position she struck the water but all agree that she was probably drowned, pulled under by the weight of her parachute. It was a wooden and cloth construction, weighing well over 30lbs.

Quoting a seaman on duty at Roath Docks who reported:

"I am in a position to know with certainty of her fate. From aloft on our steamer I distinctly saw, with the aid of glasses (binoculars) the parachute fall flat over her. A few minutes after, nothing could be seen of the parachute or the girl."

There were many letters to the newspapers. One from H.M. Inspector of Schools

The fateful descent

calling for a total ban on balloon ascents. Others calling for the immediate imprisonment of Mr Gaudron for allowing so young a girl to risk her life for his profit.

The balloon was found half buried in the mud near the mouth of the River Rhymney, a couple of miles east of Cardiff Docks. This was an area of heavy wooden stakes hammered into the sea bed to support large fishing nets, and it was thought that the luckless girl possibly still attached to her parachute, had become tangled in the netting. The location was seached using grappling irons but to no avail. The whole area of Cardiff across the Bristol Channel as far as Clevedon on the Somerset side, as far east as the mouth of the River Ebbw near Newport was searched. Steamers, tugboats, fishermen in rowing boats, pleasure yachts from Penarth Yacht Club, they all joined in the hunt without success.

Louisa Maud Evans memorial
Bereavement Services

Three days after her disappearance what appeared to be clothing was spotted by fishermen at Nash, east of Newport. Accompanied by a Police Constable, they set off to investigate. It was Mlle Albertina. Her body was brought ashore, easily recognisable by her dress, a torn and mud-encased sailor suit.

Mlle Albertina was of course her chosen Nom de Guerre. It wasn't until a search was made of her effects that the truth was revealed. A letter was found at her lodgings with the address 'Crink's Tea Gardens' Bristol. Reporters questioned Mrs Crinks the owner, and it transpired that the unfortunate girl was the daughter of a travelling woman named Evans. When the child was only 16 months old her mother, of whom all trace had been lost, asked the Crinks to look after the baby girl. She became known as Louie Crinks but her real name was Maud Evans. It was under this name that she was buried in Cathays Cemetery, her tombstone paid for by public subscription.

Newspapers, then as now, worry every last detail from a story and in doing so they contacted Redruth in Cornwall to enquire about Mlle Albertina's previous parachute descents. There weren't any. True enough Mr Gaudron had employed a female balloonist, a Miss Alma Beaumont, but she had left to get married. A far less dangerous occupation!

Maud Evans changed her name to Mlle Albertina and took he place at the Cardiff Exhibition. The first, and sadly the last, descent of a brave, if foolhardy, young lady.

Balloon Man

The School minibus turned through the Cemetery gates. Paul Williamson, History Teacher at Willows Comprehensive, directed the driver to a rather overgrown, nondescript grave.

"Sir. What are we doing here? It's pouring down."

"Thanks for the weather report, Susan."

She shrugged and continued texting her boyfriend. Mr. Williamson stood up and walked to the front of the bus.

Capt Earnest Willows headstone
Gordon Hindess

"OK Year 7. This is the starting point of your first History lesson of the new term."

"It's scary Sir. Full of dead people and those big black birds."

"Rooks, Simon. Only rooks and jackdaws."

"They looks like vultures to me, Sir. I seen them on the telly."

"All out. The rain has eased. I know this will be a terrible ordeal for you but please leave your phones on the bus."

Out they got and stood in a desolate group around their teacher. Leah worried about the rain on her hair. Simon keeping a watchful eye on those circling crows. As for Wayne best not to even imagine where his mind was.

"Right, pay attention. This gravestone. What's the name on it? Whose it in memory of?"

"Willows Sir. Like our School Sir."

"That's right Cerys. What's his full name? What else does the stone tells us?"

"That it's raining again, Sir?"

"Apart from that, Leah. Write down all the details. Then back on the bus."

"OK Listen up. Find out all you can about our Mr. Willows. Use your laptops. Go to the Central Library, they've got filmed copies of past newspapers. Use any resources you can think of. Then two weeks from today tell me all about Mr. Willows. Just remember you have to imagine I know absolutely nothing about him."

The Earnest Willows pub
Eric R Fletcher

Mr. Williamson walked into his Year 7 Classroom. First History Lesson of the week. He was surprised to see

Willows Airship at East Moors "A magnificent flying machine"
Picture courtesy the National Museums and Galleries of Wales

that his desk had been dragged to the back of the room, to be replaced by a table, behind which stood Omah and Cerys, facing their classmates.

"Here Sir. You're sitting with us today."

Everyone except Cerys sat down. She picked up her printed notes and began.

"Our School's called Willows Comp. Not far away is Willows Avenue. And there's even a pub called 'The Ernest Willows'. So who was this man and what did he do? Why was he famous but now almost forgotten?"

Earnest Willows with his second airship in 1909
Courtesy of Cardiff Capital Collection

She clicked on her laptop and a grainy photograph of a short rather ordinary man was projected on to the wall-mounted large screen.

"His full name was Ernest Thompson Willows. He followed his father and trained as a dentist, but in 1901 he chucked that in and set up a workshop on East Moors a mile or so away. Although he had no engineering experience he began to experiment in 'lighter than air' balloon travel. After a few years his sausage-shaped balloons could be seen on their first tethered flights. Then in June 1905, he began to take short powered flights, using motor bike engines to power the propellers. The Western Mail said his first airship – he called it *Willows 1* – was 74 feet long with a diameter of 18 feet. I asked my Grampy and he reckons that's about 22 metres by 5 or 6. It weighed over 600 lbs."

Cerys changed the picture to one showing Ernest Willows standing proudly by *Willows 1*.

"Most local people thought he was mad and he'd end up killing himself. A couple of important people, somebody called Viscount Tredegar, who was the Earl of Plymouth, and Lord Ninian Crichton-Stuart. Names like that they must have been important."

[Her classmates, joined by Mr. Williamson, laughed.]

"Anyway they offered £50 to the first person to fly over Cardiff in a powered balloon. On 4 June 1910, Ernest Willows took off from East Moors, Splott and headed for the City Hall. He landed safely on the grass where the fountain is today and collected his prize money."

Again the computer changed to show a large crowd outside the City Hall as *Willows 1* came in to land.

Willows Airship outside City Hall, 1910
Courtesy of Cardiff Capital Collection

"A week later he repeated the flight to raise funds for the Infirmary in Newport Road. The next month, July 1910, he was back in the news flying from Cheltenham back to Cardiff. Took him about 4 hours. My mother's new boyfriend worked that out at about 14 miles per hour."

"The next month he set a British record for the longest journey by balloon. He flew from Cardiff to London, took him about ten hours, during that flight he became the first to fly over the Bristol Channel. He had to come down to ground level to ask people the way. A surprised railway man told him to follow the rail tracks which took him to his destination, the Crystal Palace, London. There is a photo in the newspaper showing him flying over St. Paul's Cathedral."

The picture on the screen changed to show the newspaper article.

"Always short of cash, Willows had no government or local funding so the chance to win £2,000 for the first man to fly from Paris to London really appealed to him. He renamed his balloon *The City of Cardiff* and set off in the opposite direction, London to Paris."

Cerys shuffled her papers, smiled at her classmates and sat down. Mr. Williamson stood up and applauded an embarrassed Cerys.

"Brilliant. Well done. Such confidence and clarity. First class."

She sat down. Now it was the turn of Omah.

"The balloon took off from London, David Lloyd George and Winston Churchill, they were politicians I think, anyway they were part of a very large crowd on a November afternoon to see Ernest Willows and his mechanic, Frank Godden, start their flight to Paris. It was not an easy journey. Thick fog over the English Channel was the first problem. Then a ventilator belt came off its pulley. Mr. Willows had to clamber up on to the balloon to fix it, all this in the dark. They lost their maps – Godden, the mechanic, accidentally dropped them over the edge of the basket. The petrol froze in the engine and they lost most of their oil.

"They were forced to land about 150 miles from Paris. French customs tried to charge him £30 import duty on his fuel. Willows so did not need these problems. They reached Paris, by a succession of short hops, on December 28th. That's about 8 weeks after landing on French soil. He did a few exhibition flights, usually around the Eiffel Tower and talked of returning to London by air and claiming the £2000 prize money. But he decided it would be too dangerous and he brought his balloon back to Cardiff by land. There were no crowds, no welcome home parties, just a couple of local newspaper reporters. An appeal for money to help Mr. Willows was met with little enthusiasm. He tried to raise money by exhibiting one of his balloons, charging a couple of pence to view it. That's how bad things were. He was forced to rely on pleasure trips, just up and down below a tethered balloon."

Omah cleared his throat and continued.

"October 1921 he was living in an old two-masted hulk tied up on the banks of the River Thames. His reputation took a further nose-dive when his balloon broke away from its moorings and crashed into the house of an important Australian diplomat filling every room with poisonous gas. His anger and disappointment were made worse the following year when an airman from Norway became the first to fly by balloon over the North Pole. Mr. Willows said if the British Government had done its job properly and supported him, that airman could have been him. His last headline, sadly one of his biggest, came on August 3, 1926. He was giving exhibition flights at a County show in Bedfordshire when he was killed, along with four others. The basket came apart from the gas bag and fell to the ground. Ernest Willows was found below the wreckage. His neck broken."

Omah changed the picture on the screen to show people crowding around the fallen basket. Followed by a second picture of a large crowd at his funeral in Cathays Cemetery.

Omah sat down. Mr. Williamson was on his feet, hands clapping, face smiling.

"Well done Omah, well done Cerys. Well done all of you. That was very good. 'A's all round."

The whole class was standing applauding themselves, 'high 5s' everywhere.

"Hey Sir, you gotta admit that was mint."

"Yes Wayne. It certainly was. Brilliant."

Mr. Williamson helped his class put the desks back. Today had been one of those days, sadly rare, when he was glad he had become a teacher.

Eric R Fletcher

All characters in this article with the exception of Ernest Willows, his father and his mechanic are fictional. Any resemblance to other people living or past is purely coincidental.

CHAPTER ELEVEN

Boxers

The boxers, Jim Driscoll and Jack Peterson, were of different generations and plied their pugilistic trade at different weights. Apart from being buried in Cathays Cemetery, it might be thought that they had little in common. Even their graves are in different parts of the cemetery, a reflection on their different religious persuasions, while their memorials exhibit different styles. The phrase "retired featherweight champion of the world" on Jim's memorial leaves you in no doubt that he was a boxer, but there is nothing on Jack's to even hint at this.

Jim Driscoll memorial
Gordon Hindess

Their routes into boxing were quite different. Jim acquired his boxing skills in the fairground booths. At the age of seventeen, he was earning a sovereign a week from boxing, plus a bonus of a silver crown if anyone failed in the promoter's challenge to hit the courageous Driscoll on the nose inside a minute, while the teenager's hands were tied behind his back. The prize offered for success was a sovereign, but few won it, so Jim collected many bonuses. Jack's father had wanted him to be a doctor, but instead he learned to box in a gym above a pub in the docks. After enjoying an excellent amateur career, Peterson decided that big money was available in the heavyweight division.

However, in other respects, they had much in common: they were both worthy champions, outright winners Lonsdale belts and hugely respected within the profession. In addition, their reputations were enhanced by their activities outside the ring.

Jim was a master of defence yet could mix it with the best of them. He could slip the best punches of his opponents, but respond with a lethal straight left. He won the British featherweight title in 1906 and took the Empire title in 1908. In America he set about beating the best that they had to offer, leading to a bout with the then World Champion, Abe Atell. However, Atell would only fight in a ten round no-decision contest. The fight went ahead in February 1910. The rules stated that if a boxer was not knocked out then the fight was declared a no-decision, but observers reckoned that Jim had won every round.

It was customary, for betting purposes, for the ringside reporters to give their decision as to who had won the fight and Jim was their unanimous choice. They also awarded him the accolade of Peerless Jim, a title that stayed with him thereafter.

Jim was offered a return fight with the world title at stake but had promised to box in an exhibition bout in Cardiff, in aid of his favourite charity, the Assault at Arms Committee, which supported Nazareth House, where the Sisters of Nazareth cared for scores of orphans. He effectively gave up his chance to become a world champion to honour the promise he had given. When the First World War broke out, Jim joined up and did not box professionally for six years. He attempted a come back after the war, unable to resist the lure of a last big payday, but he was not a well man and suffered two of only three defeats in his career of more than fifty fights.

While Jack was an accomplished heavyweight, he was never given a world-title shot. Many thought that he could have won world honours at his more natural weight, light heavy, but the potential rewards for heavyweights were greater. His talent took him a long way, but he tended to get into wars and soaked up a lot of punishment. This led to his retirement at the early age of twenty-five, due to persistent eye problems. Despite a relatively short career, he was the first person to hold both the British Heavyweight and Light Heavyweight titles, which he won within fifty days in 1931. He made eight successful defences of the heavyweight title and was successful in thirty-five out of his thirty-eight professional bouts.

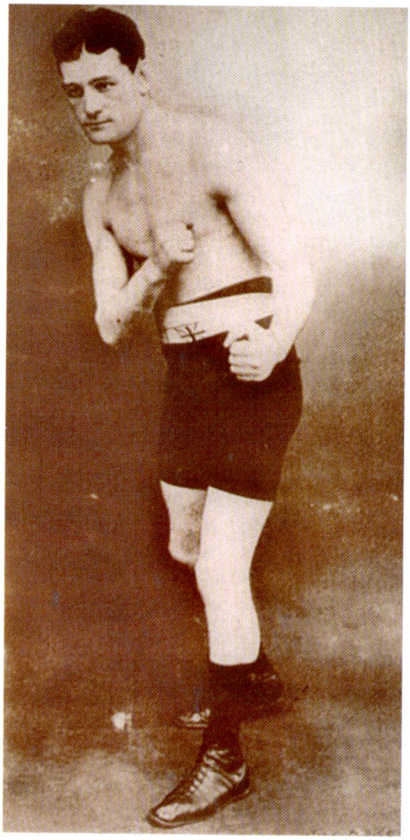

Peerless Jim Driscoll
from "Memories of Cardiff's Past" by permission of the author, Dennis Morgan

Jim Driscoll's boxing career ended in 1921, after he had been battered for 16 rounds by Charles Ledous, of France. Within five years he was dead. He died at the Duke of Edinburgh Hotel, which he kept, on the corner of Ellen Street. This is the street where he had been born and raised and he had remained close to his community, been a staunch supporter of his church and maintained great affection for the Nazareth House Orphanage. On 3 February 1925, an estimated 100,000 people lined the streets as the cortege made its way from St Paul's Church in the docks to the cemetery. In North Road the coffin was transferred from the bearers' shoulders to a gun carriage. The band of the 2nd Battalion of the Welch Regiment moved to the head of the procession, now over a mile long, while soldiers of the regiment carried their rifles reversed in honour of a dead comrade. Children from Nazareth House carried striking floral wreaths in honour of their supporter and patron. At the conclusion of a brief graveside service in the gathering dusk, the Last Post was sounded. The discerning will have noted that the official record does not support the inscription on the memorial (featherweight champion of the world), but the memorial also records that it was "erected by Nazareth House in grateful remembrance" and this perhaps explains this economy with the truth.

In contrast, Jack Peterson had a long and purposeful life after the end of his career in the ring. His many achievements included becoming the President of the British Boxing Board of Control, being awarded an O.B.E. in 1978, serving on the Sports Council for Wales and becoming the first Chairman of the Welsh Ex-Boxers Association. For many years, the British Boxing Board of Control had their headquarters in Jack Petersen (note the alternative spelling, which appears in many references) House, in London, and this provides an interesting postscript to his story. In 2001, the Board had to sell these headquarters to avoid bankruptcy when they were ordered to pay the disabled fighter, Michael Watson, more than £400,000 in damages for the injuries suffered in his fight with Chris Eubank ten years previously. And where did the Board move to? Well, Cardiff, of course: they are now in the Old Library, in Trinity Street. On his headstone, Jack is identified by his given name of John Peterson, so it would be easy to pass his grave without linking it to the renowned boxer.

Jack Peterson memorial

Gordon Hindess

But Jim Driscoll's name still lives on in the Royal Oak Hotel in Newport Road, Cardiff. Until recently, the Jim Driscoll Gym was housed upstairs and there is still an area packed with memorabilia of the famous pugilist. This had been collected by Kitty Burns, a relative of Jim's who had followed him into the Duke of Edinburgh Hotel, before moving everything to the Royal Oak in 1946.

Gordon Hindess

CHAPTER TWELVE

Leg of Male

There are the famous alongside the infamous. The good alongside the not so good. The law abiding next to the criminal, next to the taxpayer, next to the fraudster. Of course this variety and juxtaposition of burials is common to all large cemeteries, as is the unusual, the unexpected. If a prize were to be given for the strangest, the most quirky, interment in Cathays it would have to be awarded to Samuel Chivers, vinegar manufacturer, of Richmond Road, Cardiff.

The burial took place on April 16th, 1883. A week or so earlier Mr. Chivers had been involved in a serious accident, knocked over by a runaway horse and cart. He was badly injured; the heavily laden cart ran over one of his legs resulting in its amputation. And that is what was buried on that Monday in 1883. Just his leg.

Presumably Mr. Chivers hoped to be reunited with his severed limb sometime in his distant future. The years passed, perhaps he got so accustomed to the wooden replacement he forgot about the real one buried in Cathays.

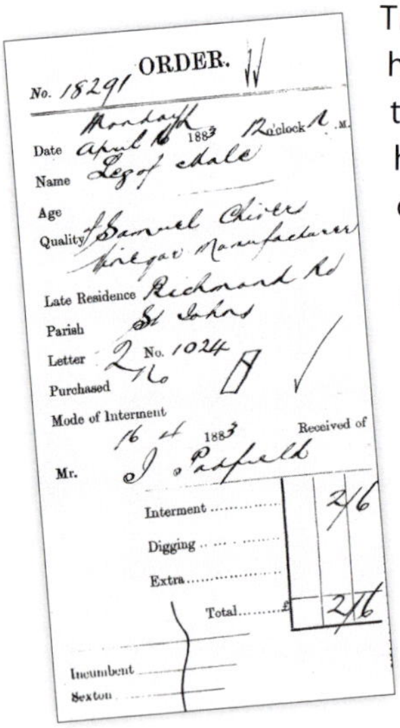

No. 18291 ORDER.

Date Monday April 16 1883 12 o'clock A.M.

Name Leg of Male

Age

Quality Samuel Chivers Vinegar Manufacturer

Late Residence Richmond Rd

Parish St Johns

Letter 2 No. 1024

Purchased

Mode of Interment

16 4 1883 Received of

Mr.

Interment 2/6

Digging

Extra

Total £ 2/6

Incumbent

Sexton

Receipt for Samuel Chivers' leg

Or perhaps what had seemed a good idea at the time just lost its appeal. As Mr. Chivers did not purchase the original plot it was, without doubt, used for other burials. A very common practice at that time. Infant mortality was so high that it was not unusual for over a dozen unrelated children to be buried together in the same unmarked grave.

A few years after the accident he moved with his ever-expanding family, Mrs Chivers, twelve children plus a cook and domestic servants to Llandough, near Penarth.

On his death in his early eighties, he was buried in a local Penarth cemetery, a dozen or so miles from Cathays and his leg.

Eric R Fletcher

CHAPTER THIRTEEN

Findlay 417

In the shelter of the tower to the right of the photograph are two ladies, obviously of high social standing, certainly not servants, Castle staff or outsiders; members of the public could not wander into the grounds from the street, as now. The Castle was then in the private ownership of the Bute family; so perhaps they are the wife of the Marquis and one of his daughters, or possibly they are both daughters, sisters taking a stroll around their father's grounds. I wonder what they are talking about, perhaps they are complaining about the difficulty of keeping the hems of their dresses, white would not seem a good choice, free from mud; or the latest London fashions. Nothing changes so maybe their talk is of young men, possible future suitors. Obviously we just don't know. Also the ramrod, standing to attention, pose of the uniformed gate-keeper (left of the open Castle gates) implies these ladies are of some importance.

Cardiff Castle entrance lodge circa 1880

Courtesy of Cardiff Capital Collection

Let's leave the ladies and concentrate on the gate-keeper. His name was William Findlay and as his upright posture suggests, he was a military man. Born Westminster, London in 1815 (the year of the Battle of Waterloo) it appears that William was taken to India by his father who was a serving soldier with the 46th Regiment of Foot. Young William, only aged 11, illegally joined his father's Regiment near Hyderabad in 1826. In 1833 when aged 18 and still stationed in India, he was promoted to drummer boy No. 417.

William Findlay had a very healthy disregard for military authority, that coupled with a propensity for enjoying himself, led to many a run in with the higher echelons of Army life. This led to two periods of imprisonment, both whilst stationed in Ireland, both in 1835. The first for eleven days, the second eight days. Not long sentences but coupled with a deduction of a penny a day from his pay for two years and six months forfeiting of beer allowance made them much more severe.

Two years later and his Regiment was in Gibraltar and again his pay was lowered by a penny a day, this time for 6 months. Excessive drinking being the reason. However by 1841 his conduct must have improved because he was given a badge to wear on his uniform denoting good behaviour.

After Gibraltar, William was posted to the West Indies. Again good boy/bad boy syndrome. August 1842 awarded a penny a day for good conduct only for it to be taken away, along with his good conduct medal, in December of the same year.

William Findlay in the 1850s
Courtesy of Hugh Payne (descendent of William Findlay)

As is often the case give a person some authority and their behaviour improves; this is what happened after his promotion to Corporal in March 1844. The Regiment was moved to Canada and William was given a second good conduct medal. This one he did not lose and in September 1846 William Findlay was again promoted this time to the rank of Sergeant.

His Regiment, the 46th of Foot, returned to the United Kingdom in 1848. William was then aged 33. 1858 they were back in Ireland and that year saw him given the rank of Colour Sergeant. On their return there followed a year at barracks in Windsor after which William was discharged to serve in the Glamorganshire Militia. In 1858 he moved to Cardiff with Elizabeth his new wife. His rebel rousing past now well behind him,

William Findlay in the 1870s
Courtesy of Hugh Payne (descendent of William Findlay)

William was in charge of drilling the Royal Glamorgan Light Infantry of Militia. He appears to have been very successful in his new post as his services were recognised by the presentation of a gold watch and chain by his Commanding Officer. His popularity continued and four years later, 1859, a silver snuff box closely followed by a silver cup given by the Officers and men of the 10th Glamorgan Rifle Volunteers.

By the early 1860s he is living in Cardiff Castle Lodge. There he stayed as Lodge Gatekeeper and Porter until his death in 1883. His first wife, Elizabeth, died in 1871. She was sixteen years older than him and is buried in Cathays Cemetery. Her tombstone reads:

Elizabeth. Wife of William Findlay.
Lodge Gatekeeper at Cardiff Castle

He married a second time, his new wife was almost 30 years younger than him. They had four children. The first two, twins, died at 1 day old. They are interred with William in an unmarked grave at Cathays. The other two, a boy and a girl survived well into adulthood.

Returning to the two ladies in the photograph, they probably lie beneath a large imposing marble edifice, whilst William is in an unmarked plot in Cathays Cemetery. I know which I would have preferred to have met and spent time with.

Eric R Fletcher

CHAPTER FOURTEEN

From Children's Games to Spies

War Games

I always seemed to be an indian, just an ordinary indian, never chosen to be the chief. Never picked as a cowboy, that's what I really hoped for. They always seemed to win whether it was just a local skirmish or, if there were enough of us, a full-scale war. Somebody like Buffalo Bill or one of those from the Saturday morning films, Roy Rogers or Gene Autry, now that would have been good.

Running between the gravestones, hitting our sides to encourage our make-believe horses, crawling through the long grass, sheltering from imaginary bullets fired from imaginary rifles by pretend cowboys. I seem to think we were Apaches or was it Cheyenne. Can't remember. It was such a long time ago, pre-junior school, pre-work, pre-marriage, pre-children, pre-retirement. So long ago it feels like pre-life.

On a good evening there would be as many as a dozen of us, all boys, no squaws or cowgirls allowed, waiting for the gates to be locked and cemetery keeper to leave his hut, put on his cycle clips and ride away up Allensbank Road. There were no railings then, the original ones had been taken away for something my grandfather called 'The War Effort'. They would not be replaced for over 25 years. So over the wall we went. The cowboys running to re-claim their stronghold from the previous game. Us indians spreading out waiting to attack.

Cowboy stronghold...
Gordon Hindess

It would be almost dark before we decided to leave, not brave enough to stay any later. To a seven-year-old cemeteries after nightfall can be spooky places.

Sometimes as we clambered over the wall we would catch sight of a young couple hurriedly climbing over in the other direction, the man more often than not in soldier's uniform. With the innocence of children we wondered where they were going. Surely they were too old to play cowboys and indians.

... or Bishop Hedley Tomb
Gordon Hindess

The Bishop

Dr John Cuthbert Hedley, Roman Catholic Bishop of Newport and Menevia, a very large diocese covering all Wales, Monmouthshire and the County of Herefordshire. He died in Cardiff in 1915, aged 78. The then Marquis of Bute provided him with a large house on the outskirts of the city in Llanishen, complete with private chapel where Bishop Hedley would daily celebrate Mass. Most Sundays his Lordship would address the faithful of the neighbourhood. Quoting from his obituary:

> *'As one listened to the white-haired Bishop in the solemn silence of that little chapel, one felt that here was a man who with heart and soul held fast to the truths of his religion and of his message. It was one of the things that most impressed one about the Bishop – the feeling he gave of his deep-rooted belief in the crystal clearness of his faith, the undimmed serenity of his confidence in the truth of all that he taught and in all that he believed'.*

He was a theologian and writer of international standing, gaining a reputation for the touching simplicity of his sermons, whilst his funeral orations had an almost poetic beauty.

No excuse is needed for including his panegyric at the double funeral of his close friends, Colonel and Mrs Vaughan. They tragically died within hours of each other. In a letter the Bishop wrote:- It is a blessed thing that good and faithful souls who have been together in life, in death should not be divided. The two coffins stood together before the altar. Dr. Hedley preached:-

> *"Death is a herald, a preacher, an apostle. He can awaken echoes in a human breast that no other voice can reach. No resolution, no philosophy, no reason can prevent a contraction of the innermost tissues of being when the toll of the bell strikes the ear, or the gloom of his pall sweeps by. Every man's life is a warning, and every man's career is a lesson. A good lesson, a moving example, a pathetic warning we shall find in the memory of John Vaughan and of Mary his wife."*

A beautiful example of late Victorian religious oratory.

Scavenging Dogs

Eight or nine years before those young boys had climbed over the cemetery walls to their make-believe world of the American west, Cardiff had been a victim of a much more serious war, heavy German bombing in the 1940s caused much damage, disruption and loss of life. During the six years of World War II over 350 people were killed by enemy air raids in Cardiff. The total for Wales was almost 1,000 with over 1,200 injured.

Owing to its status as a port this was to be expected, coal was desperately needed to keep our battleships, minesweepers, at sea. Not only Cardiff docks but also the railways on which the coal was brought down from the South Wales valleys to the waiting ships became prime targets.

One of the heaviest bombing raids on Cardiff was on May 18th, 1943, that was the night that a stick of high explosive bombs fell on Allensbank Road, they were probably meant for Maindy Army Barracks just across the road from the Heath Hotel. The elderly licensee, her daughter and son-in-law luckily had taken cover in their Anderson shelter and although it was buried by the collapsed walls of their public house, they were dug out unharmed. The dozen or so houses next to the Heath Hotel also suffered serious damage, miraculously without any loss of life. It was during that raid when a land-mine fell on Cathays Cemetery. It was probably meant for the main coal-transporting railway line which ran along what is now the busy Eastern Avenue.

As you enter the Cemetery from Allensbank Road just up from Clodien Avenue, there is a large space almost devoid of memorials, this is the area where that land-mine fell. There were reports that a local lady, on returning to her house after the 'all clear' had sounded, found a large segment of memorial stone on her mother's bed. There were also stories that the graves were exposed to such a degree that dogs were seen scavenging for bones and were reputedly spotted running up Allensbank Road with human remains in their mouths.

That raid was considered to be not only one of the heaviest that Cardiff suffered but also the best planned. Not just haphazard, indiscriminate bombing but aimed at selected targets of strategic importance. The Civil Defence controller was of the opinion that it had been thought out by somebody who knew Cardiff, someone who had lived and worked in the city before the war. It wasn't long before they came up with a name KUHEMANN: Herr Henri Kuhemann. He was Managing Director of The Flattmann Drill Company. Just a few hundred yards from Cathays Cemetery, a German-owned business based in Allensbank Road producing pneumatic drills. Herr Kuhemann had been placed there by his country's intelligence service. Four years from the autumn of 1935 up to a few days before the declaration of war he was Hitler's No. 1 spy in Wales. After the war a timber importer took over the factory, that has since been demolished and replaced by a tower block to accommodate nurses from the nearby University Hospital.

British Intelligence knew of his spying activities and his movements were followed by the police special branch. For some reason they took no action. Much information was passed to the authorities by a Mr. Herbert Steer, Company Secretary at the Flattmann factory. He reported on Herr Kuhemann's frequent trips around South Wales and the Midlands, his numerous, ostensibly for pleasure, flights from the old Cardiff airfield at Pengam. Kuhemann appears to have been allowed complete freedom to carry out his spying missions, not only was he a keen photographer but he also built up a large postcard collection of South Wales buildings, bridges and roads etc. These were soon in the hands of the Nazi Intelligence Service.

It would be reassuring to think that Herbert Steer, the Company Secretary had been recruited by our Intelligence Service and placed at the factory to keep tabs on Herr Kuhemann. A spy, spying on the spy.

Henry Kuhemann was an enthusiastic member of both the Cardiff and Newport branches of the Nazi Party, also frequently travelling to Birmingham to attend their party meetings. He was an extremely sociable man, especially when playing Mine Host at meetings of the Anglo/German Society. Those gatherings always ended with a toast being proposed to the Führer and the Fatherland accompanied by shouts of Sieg Heil after which the wine glasses were ceremoniously thrown into the fireplace and smashed. An activity which resulted in many hotels banning their future meetings.

In his office at Allensbank Road pride of place was given to photographs of Herr Kuhemann alongside Hitler and Ribbentrop, the German Ambassador to Great Britain. Still the authorities did nothing.

Herr Kuhemann and his wife hurriedly left Cardiff one morning in late August, a few days before war was declared. They told Mr Steer they were going into town shopping but in reality they were driven to the Germany Embassy in London, any incriminating papers burnt, then along with fellow countrymen on to the east coast and the sea journey home.

Many years later the guide books, flying instructions etc issued to Luftwaffe pilots came to light, these illustrated how important the photographs and intelligence gathered by Henri Kuhemann had been to the Nazi war machine.

Herr Kuhemann survived the war and it is reputed that he had the audacity in the 1960s to contact his old Company Secretary asking for help to move back to Cardiff. They destroyed the letter.

Eric R Fletcher

CHAPTER FIFTEEN

Nonconformist Ministers

The 19th century saw an amazing growth in nonconformist religion and Cardiff was in the van at this time. This chapter looks at two of the significant figures in this movement, for whom Cathays Cemetery is their final resting place.

Reverend Alfred Tilly 1821 - 1905

In the latter half of the 19th century 'Tilly of Cardiff' was a household name throughout the Baptist denomination. He commenced his pastoral life in Bridgnorth where he served for 11 years from 1846. He became pastor of Bethany, Cardiff on January 1st 1857 where he ministered until 31st March 1861.

The rapidly increasing population of the town brought to him a sense of duty to provide for the religious needs outside the central area. To the west of Cardiff the Revd Tilly had been instrumental in 1858 in establishing a Baptist Church in the Canton district. Eastward the number of inhabitants in Roath had doubled in 10 years, but was served only by a Roman Catholic Church and a mission hall in Ivor Street. In 1861 the Revd Tilly formed a new Church, 'Tredegarville' located today in The Parade. The first meeting place was above a stable in Castle Road, now called City Road. Sometimes the movement of the horses below could be heard during the service.

Within three months a permanent site was found and by 3rd December a schoolroom occupying the whole basement of the new church was opened, followed in May 1862 by the new chapel. With the support of his close friends John and Richard Cory the full cost of £3600 was paid within four years.

Led by the Revd Tilly, Baptist churches were opened in Grangetown, Longcross Street, Pearl Street, Splott Road, Maindy, Rumney, Llanishen and Cathays Terrace in Cardiff, and beyond – English Baptist chapels being opened in Caerphilly and Tondu.

Alfred Tilly memorial and detail of inscription
Gordon Hindess

In addition to his work as a pastor, the Revd Tilly served 30 years on the Committee of the Baptist Missionary Society, and for many years served the interests of Cardiff Infirmary, the School Board and the University College of South Wales and Monmouthshire.

Through his influence and the generosity of his friend, Mr John Cory, the Livingstone Inland Mission was founded and the pioneer missionary sent out on the suggestion of the Revd Tilly.

The grave of the Revd Tilly is located alongside the path a few steps west from the Cemetery Chapels.

Rumney Baptist chapel in Cardiff is named 'The Alfred Tilly Memorial Church' and thanks are extended to the present day minister, the Revd Stewart Ryce Davies, for the information on which this article is based.

Reverend John Pugh 1846 - 1907

John Pugh, founder and Superintendent of the Calvinistic Methodist Forward Movement passed away at 11pm Palm Sunday, 24 March 1907, leaving behind a memorial to the wondrous works of God.

Pugh was born in 1846 in New Mills, Montgomeryshire to parents who were members of the local Calvinistic chapel. At the age of 14 years he joined his father, as his clerk, in Pembrokeshire where he was working as a contractor for David Davies, of Llantarnam, who was building the Tenby Railway. There he came under the ministry of Mr Thomas Charles Edwards, to whom John Pugh attributed his conversion. He entered Trevecca College in 1869 and left three years later, taking up the pastorate of a small church in Park Place, Tredegar in Monmouthshire. While at Tredegar God burdened him for the non-welsh speaking population of industrial South Wales and starting in Tredegar he commenced a work, which under God, was to have a resounding effect on the whole of Wales. Despite opposition the membership of the church in Tredegar had so increased that by 1876, when he moved to Pontypridd, a new building seating 700 had been built

As in Tredegar, Pugh faced opposition from within his congregation and from the vested interests in Pontypridd. However he persevered and the work grew as before; by 1883 a larger church had to be built. In 1889 he left Pontypridd to take up the pastoral care of the Clifton St Church, in Splott, Cardiff. It was here that he came face to face with a task far greater than anything that he had encountered before. Cardiff was in the middle of rapid expansion; its population in 1881 was 82,000 and soared to 164,000 by 1901. With this sudden growth and prosperity many of Pugh's contemporaries, while acknowledging the immense prosperity that was flowing into Cardiff, were concerned about the social conditions. Pugh saw that all of this was secondary to the desolate state of religion in many areas of the borough, where for a population of approximately 130,000 there was only accommodation for less than 50,000.

Pugh's first enterprise was Roath United Mission; this drew support from the other evangelical ministers in Roath and over the next two years large numbers gathered to hear Pugh preach and the Clifton Street Church almost doubled. In 1890 another work called the Prison Gate Mission commenced, which helped many discharged prisoners to turn from a life of crime and degradation. In 1891 following discussions with his friend,

Rev William Ross of Glasgow, and prayerful consideration he secured a vacant plot at the corner of Ordell and Carlisle Streets in the densely populated area of Splott and Adamsdown. He proposed to start with a tent mission and to that end he erected a tent 120 feet long and 33 feet wide. To assist him he invited Seth Joshua who had been converted under his ministry in Pontypridd. The work grew from its first day, although the tent was blown down by a gale in October 1891. A wooden hall was promptly built to replace it, which in turn was replaced by a building known as East Moors Hall in July 1892 and seated 1,000 people.

John Pugh headstone
Bill Mosley

Missions and God's blessing on the work was the pattern for the rest of his life. In 1891 two works in Canton commenced, Memorial Hall, Cowbridge Road, by St David's Hospital, and Clive Road Hall, Canton. Both grew rapidly in this crowded area.

The South Wales valleys were not ignored; beginning in 1891, in Treorchy he and his fellow evangelists commenced work. In the following year missions were held at Porth and Graig in Pontypridd; a church was built in Porth in 1894 and before long other centres were opened by Pugh's friends in Cwmparc and Pontygwaith.

In 1892 Pugh's work and vision were formally adopted by the Denomination enabling him to resign his pastorate at Clifton Street and to devote his time to the establishing of churches up and down Wales. Within the next 3 years "Forward Movement" halls were opened in Abercarn, Abertillery, Cross Keys, Ebbw Vale, and Elliot's Town in Monmouthshire, with others following at Blaina, Llanhilleth, Pontypool and Six Bells. Further missions in Glamorgan were established: at Treharris in 1894, then in Aberavon, Abercynon, Cilfynydd, Maesteg, Penrhiwceiber and Penydarren.

The larger towns of South Wales were not forgotten. In 1892 in the St Helens district of Swansea and helped by the Rev Morris Morgan the work grew and a hall was built in 1893 which by 1899 had to be replaced. At Hebron chapel in Swansea, for which Pugh had responsibility, he invited Frank Jackson to take control of the work.

In Newport in August 1895 Frank and Seth Joshua were invited to commence the work. The Temperance Hall was hired where congregations of 3000 in the morning and 500 in the afternoon met. The Temperance Hall soon became too small so the Corn Exchange was hired until the Central Hall was built in 1906. Preaching centres commenced in the Marshes in 1896: Malpas Road in 1897 and Corporation Road in 1900. Growth was not just confined to the "Forward Movement" work – two existing churches in Newport opened new branches at Caerleon Road and Stow Park. Neither was the work limited to the industrial heartlands of South Wales: in 1898 J E Ray moved from Cardiff to Wrexham, other evangelists commenced work in Barry in 1900, Neath in 1902, Morriston in 1903.

As these works were progressing Pugh turned his attention to the Cathays area of Cardiff holding meetings in hired rooms in Dalcross and Fitzroy Streets. The members of work were based in Crwys Hall, Monthermer Road, then opened a building at the junction of Harriet Street and Rhymney Street, known as the King's Way Hall. Pugh was also concerned about the children of the area of the Heath and after visiting the area he was able to purchase land opposite the Barracks field and a school hall was erected for 350 and opened on 11th November 1900. By January 1901 a church was formed and in 1903 they called Rev John Thomas, who had been Pugh's assistant in the Forward Movement, as their pastor. Under his ministry the church was opened in 1906.

When Dr Pugh died in 1907 having been faithful in much, he had been entrusted with much, being instrumental in erecting 48 places of worship in 15 years and being granted the great privilege of seeing many souls gain that "inheritance which fadeth not away!"

Ivor Lippett (Alfred Tilly)
Nicholas Davey (John Pugh)

CHAPTER SIXTEEN

Scout Hero

May 2009 was the 60th Anniversary of the sad death of a brave twelve-year-old boy. A pupil of Monkton House School and a member of the 14th Boy Scout troop – the Lord Mayor's Own. John Howard Davies lost his life in a selfless attempt to rescue a fellow scout who was in danger of drowning, caught by the rising tide whilst crossing back to the mainland from Sully Island. Lying about six miles south-westerly from Cardiff Bay, Sully Island only becomes a true island at high tide. It is small and uninhabited and can become a death-trap when the causeway becomes covered by the incoming tide.

Left: John Davies in Scout uniform

Above: John Davies in cricket flannels. John drowned the day before his 13th birthday. The cricket flannels he is wearing were an early present

The tragedy occurred when a party of scouts including John Davies left it too late to return. They were soon in difficulties with the tide rising much faster than usual due to high, almost gale-force winds. T. Rees, the Rover Scout in charge did everything possible to prevent an accident and with two exceptions the party of about ten reached safety. He then went back into the water to assist the last two boys. The tide was flooding over the causeway and Rees had great difficulty helping his two charges.

John had reached the shore when he heard their cries for help. He quickly removed his shoes and swam to help in the rescue. He reached the younger boy, his friend Michael Glossop, a non-swimmer, and managed to hold his head above the water until a rowing boat, launched by three local men, came to their assistance. Meanwhile the leader, Rover Scout T. Rees, helped the other boy but in the struggle, he too became exhausted. Margaret Vaughan, a 14-year-old schoolgirl, saw the problem they were in. She swam to them and towed the boy to the shore. He supported himself by grasping the straps of her costume. Her action saved the boy's life and possibly also that of the Scout Leader.

As the boat was almost level with John and his friend Michael, the two boys became separated and sank beneath the waves. A member of the boat's crew jumped overboard and rescued Michael. He was brought ashore unconscious and taken to Llandough Hospital nearby, from where he was discharged none the worse for his ordeal. John Davies' body was recovered days later. At the Inquest it was revealed he was not a strong swimmer – one width of the local Council pool was his limit.

The London Gazette of November 1949 carries the announcement that: The King has been pleased to award the Albert Medal to both Margaret Vaughan and the late John Davies for their gallantry. It ends: There is no doubt that in returning to the aid of his friend after he himself had reached safety, John gave his life in the rescue attempt. The Albert Medal also known as the Peoples' VC was awarded for acts of heroism in saving or endeavouring to save the lives of others.

John was also honoured by the Scout movement. He was awarded their highest accolade, the Bronze Cross. The citation reads 'IN POSTHUMOUS RECOGNITION OF HIS GREAT GALLANTRY' and is signed by Lord Rowallan, Chief Scout .

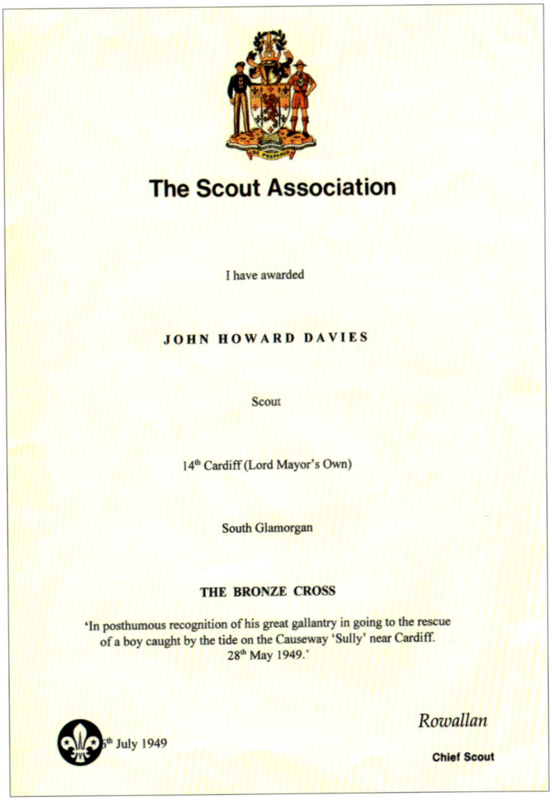

The Scout Association

I have awarded

JOHN HOWARD DAVIES

Scout

14th Cardiff (Lord Mayor's Own)

South Glamorgan

THE BRONZE CROSS

'In posthumous recognition of his great gallantry in going to the rescue of a boy caught by the tide on the Causeway 'Sully' near Cardiff. 28th May 1949.'

5th July 1949

Rowallan

Chief Scout

Above: The Scout Award Cross

Right: The Scout Association Award Certificate

THE CARNEGIE HERO FUND TRUST

IN RECOGNITION · OF THE · HEROISM · OF JOHN H. DAVIES, WHO · DIED · ON · 28th MAY · 1949 · AS · THE RESULT · OF · EFFORTS TO · SAVE · HUMAN · LIFE AT · SWANBRIDGE, GLAMS..

DUNFERMLINE .... CHAIRMAN.
28th JULY 1949. .... SECRETARY.

Left: Memorial to John Davies.
Note the use of the style of military headstones
Above: Carnegie Award Certificate

His memorial stone in Cathays Cemetery carries the Scout emblem. The Carnegie Hero Trust donated one hundred pounds to purchase the stone. There was a little surplus, enough to give a silver cup to his school, Monkton House. It was awarded annually to the boy who most improved at swimming. The School magazine in their reporting of his death finishes: We shall ever remember the heroic sacrifice, bravery and strong sense of duty of a boy whom we knew and liked.

This account is dedicated to keeping alive the memory of a brave young boy who gave his life to help others.

Eric R Fletcher

Appendix I

Names of people associated with the Cemetery in its early years

When compiling a history of a local or central government department what is often missing are lists of employees. Having had the opportunity to use the minute books for the cemetery committee, the names of the various employees who are mentioned within their pages have been extracted. The Glamorgan Record Office holds the surviving records of the Cardiff Burial Board which includes the following:- Records of the Cardiff Burial Board, 1859-1951: burial registers for Cathays cemetery, 1859-1951; registers of grants of deeds for grave spaces, 1924-1947; cash books, 1885-1935 (incomplete); ministers' fee book, 1903-1906; committee expenditure book, 1919-1925; wages books, 1887-1922; register of mortgages, 1859-1860.

Lists of Employees from the Minute books and Manager report books

Profession	Dates Mentioned
Architect	
Robert George Thomas	1859-1861
Thomas Waring	1859-1874
Surveyor	
Thomas Waring	1859-1874
T L Johnson	1874-1876
J A B Williams	1877-1878
Mr W Harpur	1890-1900
Manager/Lodge Keeper	
William Timms	1861-1867
Mr Cornelious Hatch	1867-1880
Mr Lewis	1888
Mr A Whitworth	1888-Dec 1907
Mr F Prukett	Jan 1908-February 1908
Mr C Willis	March 1908-April 1910
Mr B Rouse	May 1910 up to June 1935
Clerk	
Mr Matthews	1859-1861
Mr E P Richards	1861-1865
Mr Montague Grover	1865-1867
Mr George Salmon	1867-1875
F R Gracehill	1875- March 1905
Finance Clerk	
F R Gracehill	1874-1875

Lists of Employees from the Minute books and Manager report books *continued*

Profession	Dates Mentioned
Auditor	
D Roberts	1876-1878
Sextons/Grave Diggers/Labourers	
Michael Ryan	1872
Widow of Jeremiah Collins	1878
Thomas Pullen	1888
John McMahon	1895
James Vickery	1897
Thomas Hacker, aged 21 years	1907
George Hardage, employed for 16 years	1908
F Dale sick for 33 weeks worked only 14 weeks	1908
J Biggin, Foreman for many years	1909
G Cleterly, Gardener of many years	1909
G Carter, Gardener of many years	1909
M Batker, Cleaner	1909
William, Gardener employed for 30 years	1909
Francis Dale, employed 18 years died 10/10/1909	1909
Gate Keeper Thomas	1910
Gate Keeper Saunders	1910

Applicants for the Post of Cemetery Manager – date 12th June 1867

Thomas Chapman paid 5s for expenses
Cornelius Hatch paid £3.3s for expenses (appointed 1867, died 3rd December 1880)
Arthur Murrell paid 5s for expenses
Jenkin Rees paid 5s for expenses
Isaac Smith paid 5s for expenses.

Applicants for the Post of Cemetery Manager 1880

By contrast, when the Post became vacant in 1880 there were 105 applicants and T. Haydyn, a police constable from Cardiff, was appointed. A full list of the applicants is available from the Friends of Cathays Cemetery.

Nicholas Davey

Appendix II

Poems by Richard Garman inspired by Cathays Cemetery

Black Out

Let black be banned
no place for it here.
Let rainbow clothes
spawn rainbow thoughts.

Why be sad?
I enquire encouragingly.
Hug your neighbour.
I invite your embrace.
Greet old friends,
separated by circumstance.
Bridge those chasms
of old animosities.
Today is the beginning
of the rest of my death.

Thank you all for being with me
dressed in robes of warm compassion.
As I lie here a non-participant
casketed in my cloak of serenity,
a tight lipped smile washes over me
lighting up my black ball eyes.

Don't be saddened by my passing
we all must pass along this road.

© Richard Garman, 2nd March, 2008

Grief and Gratitude

The conveyor belt of life,
studded with precious stones,
glides inexorably onward.

Each little gem sparkles,
but the simple stones pale
in the enormity of the background.
Their absence noticed by few.

Some jewels stand proud,
bright and joyful,
larger than life,
proclaiming their place in the world.

When the grim jeweller comes,
his tweezers pluck them away.
A void is left.
The more the man
the greater the gap.

The more the man,
the greater the pride,
the happier the memories,
of the man we all loved.

© Richard Garman, 11th March, 2007

It's My Funeral

Bury me or burn me,
why should I care?
I'm the only living person
who won't be present there.

Marble kerbs and a headstone
carved like the page of a book.
An aura of solid permanence
but a glossy, self-conscious look.

Ashes are dry and soulless
remembered by only a few.
Scattered in some special place
known only to me and you.

I could be a plaque on a park bench
you might rest your back on me.
Perhaps some flowers on a lamp post
or a specially planted tree.

All these things are tangible
to be observed and measured.
I crave a subtle legacy
from the memories I've treasured.

I'd like to think there's a different way
to leave my stamp on the world
as I march on to the next one
with battle banners furled.

I may not have the influence
to change the course of the nation,
but I can leave my mark somehow
on the following generation.

I'll make my own memorial
as I live from day to day
by the way I treat my fellows
and the things I do and say.

A simple act of kindness
keeping dignity intact
is a much more solid monument
than a dramatic final act.

Dead Poetry

I can't upset dead people,
no matter how I try.
So I can write about them,
with no word of a lie.

I might upset the living,
so treat them carefully.
When I shed *my* mortal coils,
they'll have a go at me!

Appendix III

Plan of the Cemetery

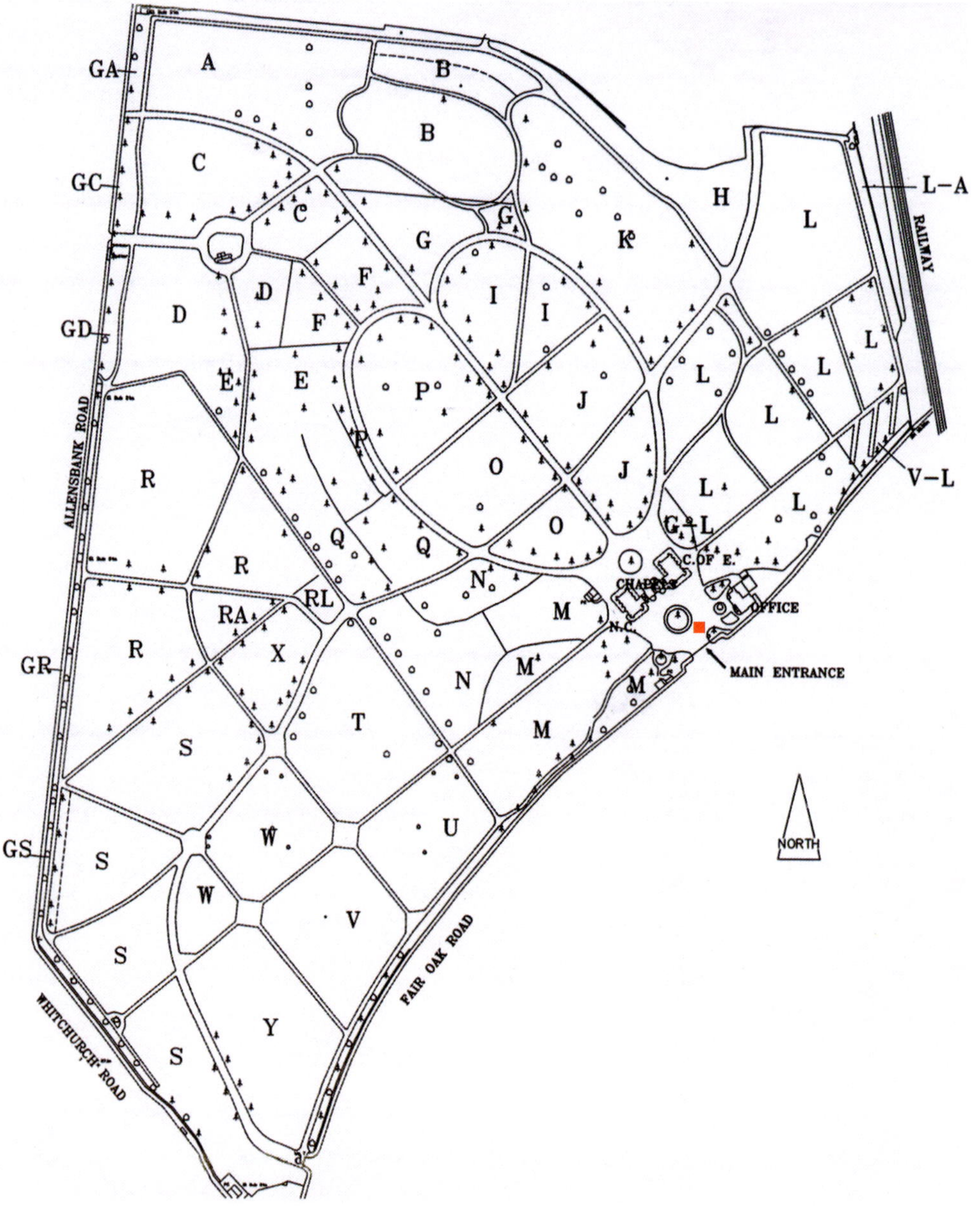

Cathays Cemetery South Plan. Information hut indicated by red square near Fairoak Road main entrance

Bereavement Services

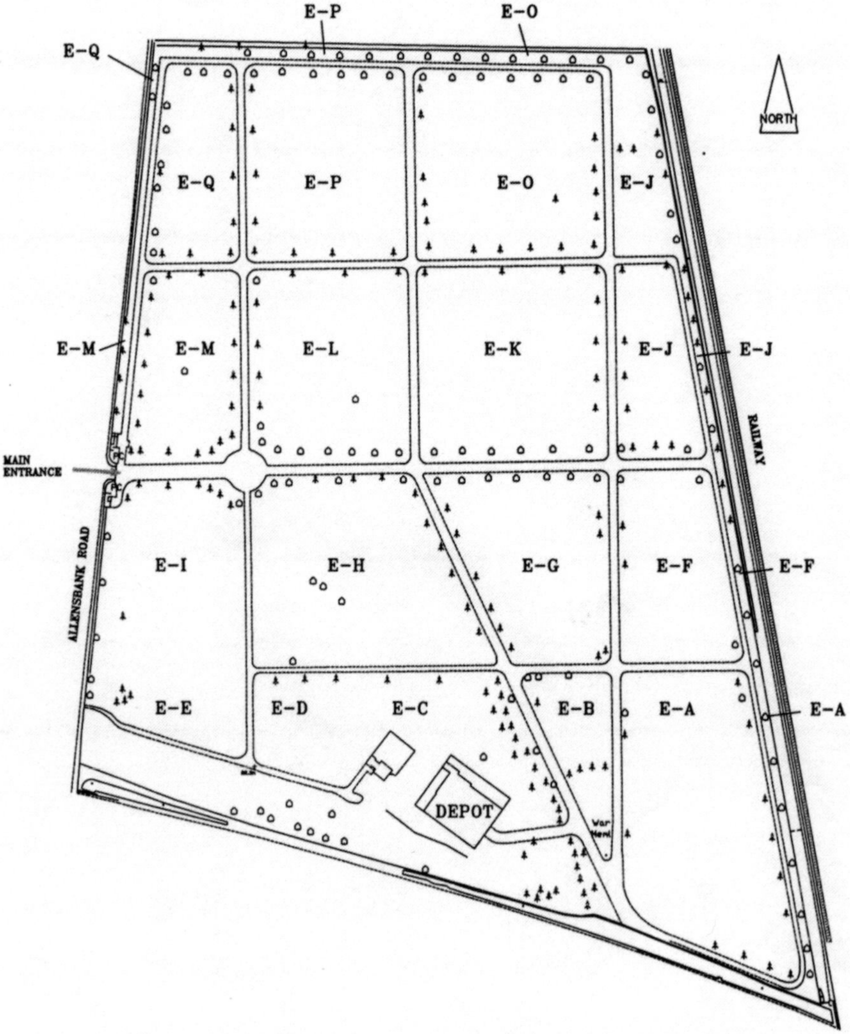

Cathays Cemetery North Plan
Bereavement Services